Sirens

THE STUDY OF SOUND

Editor: Michael Bull

Each book in The Study of Sound *offers a concise look at a single concept within the field of sound studies. With an emphasis on the interdisciplinary nature of the topics at hand, the series explores a range of core issues, debates, and objects within sound studies from a variety of perspectives and within a multitude of contexts.*

Editorial Board:

Carolyn Birdsall, Assistant Professor of Television and Cross-Media Culture, University of Amsterdam, The Netherlands

Martin Daughtry, Assistant Professor of Music, Arts and Humanities, NYU, USA

Michael Heller, Associate Professor, Department of Music, University of Pittsburgh, USA

Brian Kane, Associate Professor, Department of Music, Yale University, USA

Marie Thompson, Lecturer, School of Film and Media, University of Lincoln, UK

James Mansell, Assistant Professor of Cultural Studies, Department of Culture, Film and Media, University of Nottingham, UK

Published Titles:

The Sound of Nonsense by Richard Elliott
Humming by Suk-Jun Kim
Lipsynching by Merrie Snell
Sonic Fiction by Holger Schulze

Forthcoming Titles:

Sonic Intimacy by Malcolm James
Wild Sound by Michael Pigott

Sirens

Michael Bull

BLOOMSBURY ACADEMIC
NEW YORK • LONDON • OXFORD • NEW DELHI • SYDNEY

BLOOMSBURY ACADEMIC
Bloomsbury Publishing Inc
1385 Broadway, New York, NY 10018, USA
50 Bedford Square, London, WC1B 3DP, UK

BLOOMSBURY, BLOOMSBURY ACADEMIC and the Diana logo are
trademarks of Bloomsbury Publishing Plc

First published in the United States of America 2020

Copyright © Michael Bull, 2020

Cover design and image by Liron Gilenberg, www.ironicitalics.com

All rights reserved. No part of this publication may be reproduced or transmitted in
any form or by any means, electronic or mechanical, including photocopying, recording,
or any information storage or retrieval system, without prior permission in writing
from the publishers.

Bloomsbury Publishing Inc does not have any control over, or responsibility
for, any third-party websites referred to or in this book. All internet addresses given in
this book were correct at the time of going to press. The author and publisher regret any
inconvenience caused if addresses have changed or sites have ceased to exist, but can
accept no responsibility for any such changes.

Library of Congress Cataloging-in-Publication Data
Names: Bull, Michael, 1952- author.
Title: Sirens / Michael Bull.
Description: First edition. | New York: Bloomsbury Academic, [2020] |
Series: The study of sound | Includes bibliographical references and
index. | Summary: "From the seductive danger of the Sirens in Greek myth
to the protective/warning sounds of sirens in the 20th century, this
book investigates the paradoxical and complex meaning of sirens in
Western culture"– Provided by publisher.
Identifiers: LCCN 2019037301 (print) | LCCN 2019037302 (ebook) | ISBN
9781501305009 (hardback) | ISBN 9781501304996 (paperback) | ISBN
9781501305016 (pdf) | ISBN 9781501305023 (epub)
Subjects: LCSH: Sirens (Mythology) | Mythology, Greek.
Classification: LCC BL820.S5 .B85 2020 (print) | LCC BL820.S5 (ebook) |
DDC 398/.45–dc23
LC record available at https://lccn.loc.gov/2019037301
LC ebook record available at https://lccn.loc.gov/2019037302

ISBN: HB: 978-1-5013-0500-9
PB: 978-1-5013-0499-6
ePDF: 978-1-5013-0501-6
eBook: 978-1-5013-0502-3

Series: The Study of Sound

Typeset by Deanta Global Publishing Services, Chennai
Printed and bound in the United States of America

To find out more about our authors and books visit www.bloomsbury.com
and sign up for our newsletters.

*In memory of my good friend
Walter Harris (1925–2019)
Writer, Broadcaster and Raconteur*

CONTENTS

Siren Beginnings 1
   Sounding Out the Sirens 3

Siren Traces 13
  1 Prolegomena to the Sirens 15
  2 Eclipsing the Acousmatic: The Story of the Sirens? 18
  3 Sonic Sleepwalkers: Siren Myths from Homer, to Bach, to Nancy Sinatra 25
  4 Remembering the Forgotten Sounds of Air-Raid Sirens: *Charlie Hebdo* to Dresden and Beyond 36
  5 Urban Sirens: 9/11, Dizzee Rascal and Varese 53
  6 Timing the Sirens: Kurt Vonnegut Meets Theodor Adorno 61
  7 Siren Spaces: A Different Colonization? 67
  8 Hearing the Sirens: A Tale of Sonic Exclusivity? 76
  9 Sirens for the Young: From Fénelon to Disney 81
  10 Kafka's Sirens and the Story of Silencing 86

11 Sonic Aftermaths: Sirens and Stormy Daniels 94

12 Sonic Fallibility: Kittler's Sirens 97

Afterword: Let's Sing Another Song Boys. This One Has Grown Old and Bitter (Leonard Cohen) 108

Notes 113
Bibliography 124
Index 132

Siren Beginnings

Sounding Out the Sirens

When embarking upon writing the present volume inquisitive friends asked me what the topic of the book was. On telling them that I was writing a book on 'Sirens' some looked surprised – 'Why do you want to write a book on mermaids?' they would ask. Others would exclaim, 'Oh yes, a book on music!'. One sound scholar excitedly commented, 'Yes, a book on police sirens is just what is needed!' and so on. The book series to which this volume contributes aims to interrogate a single concept, object or issue through the lens of sound studies broadly conceived. The study of sound crosses disciplinary boundaries as does the study of Sirens. In addition to the cross-disciplinary nature of the study is a vagueness attached to both the nature of the object – a Siren – and what it signifies. The study of Sirens is beset with two significant problems; that of an intellectual division of labour encouraging specialization of topic and area; and an inherent ambiguity as to what the object of study is: the Siren/siren.[1]

Sirens in one form or another are studied widely in literature, philosophy, history, classical studies, cultural and film studies, anthropology, architecture, music, ethnomusicology and, more recently, in sound studies. The page of text in which Odysseus 'confronts' the Sirens is one of the most cited pages in Western cultural history with each age breathing new life into the sails of the Siren myth. Sirens have spawned hundreds of books and many thousands of pages of analysis over the last three thousand years. Of less interest are the more recent 'technological' sirens of urban culture – the ones that we hear in daily life. These sirens have a much shorter history than the mythical Sirens from whom they derive their name.[2] It is perhaps unsurprising that their omission from critical texts is mirrored in their relative absence in the comments made by my colleagues. The exclusion of these 'recent' sirens from critical discourse is intriguing as industrial sirens peppered the industrial landscape until relatively recently, from ship to factory, sirens have regulated the working day for many industrial workers and acted as guides for ships as they entered the ports of New York, London and elsewhere. Equally, air-raid sirens were a dominant presence in the soundscapes of cities during the Second World War and the Cold War remaining, to this day, as warnings of danger from the air but also as warnings against potential natural disasters.

Siren studies tend to reside within disciplinary boundaries rather than existing between them. For example, there is much work undertaken under the rubric of classical studies and Greek studies with book series covering writings on *Myths and Poetics* within the classical period for example. These writings rarely stray from their 'Classical' subject matter, even though they might choose to focus on the presentation of a specific area of concern such as the representation of women in the work of Homer – they rarely move beyond their period of study (Cohen 1995). Equally, there is a wealth of writings within musicology discussing Sirens and their presence within the medieval motet or their existence within opera more generally (Smart 2000; Zayaruznaya 2018). The study of Sirens/sirens takes many forms, subject to the discipline and interest of the writer, from the gendering of Sirens (Peraino 2006), to their filmic representation (Miklitch 2011) to their role in musical performance (Fleeger 2014). These studies tend to remain locked within a confining brief, even if broadly 'interdisciplinary' in choosing one 'type' of Siren over another: the study of Sirens of myth in either their classical sense or in terms of popular or/and musical culture for example. In the following chapters I demonstrate that an understanding of the multiple historical and cultural meanings of the Sirens of myths does not preclude connecting them to more recent developments in the use of industrial sirens. An interest in the sexual representation of Sirens in popular culture, for example, need not preclude an investigation into their relationship with and rationale for their use as anti-nuclear devices in contemporary Japan and Hawaii. There exists an institutional and intellectual reluctance to join these 'disparate' siren threads together and theorize their potentially overlapping meanings and significance. One has to look to the work of Theodor Adorno and Max Horkheimer in order to make this connection, even though their work on myth and reason has a broader sweep than the mere analysis of Sirens within Western culture; and even here it is necessary to extrapolate imaginatively in order to connect the Sirens of myth to the siren warnings of man-made destruction.[3] This intellectual division of labour from which

Sirens/sirens both prosper and suffer represents an intellectual division of labour from which sound studies itself is not immune.

Sound studies has largely restricted itself to the investigation of sirens that pass us by on the street while neglecting those Sirens of popular culture. Yet, even its treatment of these industrial sirens has remained, at best, partial. While it is the case that sound studies has shown a greater partiality to the vibrations of mechanical sirens to those Sirens that 'sing', it often confines its analysis to the difficulties surrounding the recognition and placing of sirens sounds emanating from the vehicles of the emergency services within the spaces of cities, often New York. This work, largely functionalist in orientation, focuses on the hearing of, and placement and design of, sirens in an attempt to improve upon and overcome obstacles to hearing. These challenges to hearing are historical, empirical and technological. How, for example, might siren warnings be heard in the seclusion of hermetically sealed automobiles, or in concreted apartment blocks or offices or in underground tube stations and so on. How might sonic information be adequately targeted at potential listeners so that they trust these warning sounds and respond appropriately (Neuhaus 2003)? These issues are alive and important and their significance is not contested here, but rather their 'reach'. The investigation of sirens might seem relatively straightforward *if* one confines the analysis to a functional appraisal of design and listening. The present book argues that we need to go further than this, both in terms of how we analyse the nature and meaning of sirens and, importantly, in extending siren analysis to include the role of Sirens in popular culture in order to cast light on their connections and differences. Hillel Schwartz in his magisterial history of noise, while not 'functional' in the least, pays little attention to sirens of either type throughout his 900-page text. His discussion of sirens takes place primarily in relation to the concerns of Noise Abatement Societies. Sirens, he correctly observes, were often perceived of as signifiers of the inexorable march of industrialization in the nineteenth and early twentieth centuries. Schwartz positions sirens at the forefront of attempts to control urban noise, 'across the last two hundred [years] we have regularly surpassed it [noise] at every point along the spectrum: sirens and steam whistles on the high end' (Schwartz 2011: 37). Elsewhere, Schwartz falls in line with the dominant debate with a series of reflections on how sirens might be sufficiently instrumentalized in a world of competing sounds. When briefly alluding to the Sirens of mythology in reference to the novels of Franz Kafka and James Joyce he restricts his discussion to the role that the First World War played in the experience of the authors rather than, for example, to the cultural and historical meanings of the gendering of Sirens in their work. This issue forms a central component in the present work.

These disciplinary issues are exacerbated by the shifting nature of meanings attached to the very study and understanding of sirens. Sirens are mythical, material and constantly metamorphizing; they are the subject of Greek myth, of Victorian hypocrisy, of male domination, the subject of film, literature and music, an essential component in the defence of citizens and cities in wartime and in times of natural disasters, they are a dialectical representative of the conflicting nature of Enlightenment thought. They represent a multiplicity of perspectives and subject matter joined by one term – siren. In daily life we confront the sirens of the emergency services, in some parts of the world remaining air-raid sirens warn of earthquakes or tsunamis. We read of aquatic creatures called sirens or mermaids, see them on screen, as paintings in art galleries, listen to the siren songs of Debussy, Dizzy Rascal or Wolf Alice.[4] This very multiplicity spawns vagueness and imprecision. Dictionary definitions do not clarify but merely compound confusion. The *Oxford English Dictionary* gives similar definitions of sirens to every other major dictionary in defining them as,

> Greek mythology. Any of several women or winged creatures, half woman half bird, whose singing was supposed to lure unwary sailors to destruction on the rocks. Formerly also a mermaid.

The Oxford definition remains ambiguous from the beginning. Are Sirens women or some other creature? Why would their song lure sailors onto the rocks? Neither is the metamorphosis of women into Sirens or later mermaids commented upon. Indeed the historical derivation is mistaken, as 'mermaids' were invented after the mythical Homeric Sirens. The dictionary definition continues:

> A woman who sings sweetly; a dangerously fascinating woman, a temptress; anything tempting or alluring.

The dictionary divides Sirens into either women who sing or who are tempting in some unspecified way. The object of this temptation is left unclear – it is not apparent whether "anything" includes mechanical sirens which emit noise or music; if so it is not clear through which technological medium this might happen. Only in the final brief definition of sirens to be used as an adjective might the two disparate sirens come together. The most confusing aspect of the dictionary definition is its rapid movement from the Sirens of Greek mythology to embodying the myth to include initially 'some women' before moving on to include *all* women as Sirens before broadening the definition to refer to *anything* that is 'tempting'. This definition exists firmly within the tropes of Western popular culture and is increasingly alluded to in Siren critical discourse which opens out the subject of siren to include almost anything. This second definition does potentially move away from the heterosexual assumption of the first by not defining who it is that is being 'tempted'. The metamorphizing of the Sirens, an issue addressed in the work of Peraino (2006) might explain its attraction, as a term, to the LGBT movement who selectively use the term organizationally.

The following and third dictionary definition of sirens remains a picture of clarity in relation to the first two definitions.

> An acoustical instrument for producing musical tones and used in numbering the vibrations in any note. A device for making a loud, prolonged or undulating sound as a signal or warning.

These sirens emit mechanical sounds, often disliked by those of the Noise Abatement Societies around the world, but are sometimes made objects of sonic nostalgia as townspeople in America sometimes campaign to have their sirens reinstated (Ross 2015).

Finally, the dictionary also uses the term as an 'adjective' to refer to anything that requires a warning – the object of which lies in the 'eye of the beholder' to refer to anything from Marshall McLuhan's view of modern culture to that of Samuel Beckett's critique of the poverty of language now resurfaced in the age of social media. The present work leaves the adjectival use of sirens to others as this dissipates the meaning of sirens to imply anything the speaker dislikes rather than the 'specifics' of mythical and material sirens.

This division of sirens into the mythical manifested as women and the technological mirrors their study in academic discourse, albeit the academic discourse is often critical of the cultural assumptions lying behind defining women thus (Cavarero 2005). Occasionally a writer might indeed cite mythical Sirens as being mechanical, not human, thus moving Sirens from one category to the other. Indeed, the association of Sirens with the beauty of song while dominant is not uncontested, even in the writings of Ancient Greece. 'He can hear[Odysseus] what no mortal has heard without dying: the scream-songs (at the same time *phthoggos* and *aoide*) of the Sirens' (Quignard 2016: 110). Medieval thought in associating Sirens with birds also draws distinctions as to the nature of their 'sounds'. This animal or 'non-human' sound surfaces occasionally in contemporary popular culture. In the 1984 Hollywood movie *Splash*, Daryl Hannah plays the *good* mermaid so beloved in popular culture from Hans Christian Andersen to the present. Hannah falls in love with Tom Hanks in the movie, coming onto land where she has been given legs for six days before she must leave or stay human forever. The film is unusual in its portrayal of the mermaid song in that when the Hannah character tries to sing, she emits a piercing shriek that shatters adjacent television screens. When her true identity as a mermaid is discovered, she returns to the sea with Hanks and both live happily ever after – not the ending that Homer's Sirens sought. It is not the song of the siren that attracts in the Hollywood movie, but the body. Elsewhere writers sometimes stray into the mechanical, the non-human, in their discussion of Sirens. Dolar in his analysis of the Kafka short story 'Silence of the Sirens' states that Kafka's Sirens, 'have no consciousness, all their behaviour is going through the motions, they are automata, they are inanimate, they are machines imitating humanity, cyborgs' (Dolar 2006: 173). Popular culture has also moved from one category to the other with cyborg women inhabiting movies from Fritz Lang's *Metropolis* (1928) to the recent *Alita Battle Angel* (2018). Not all of these cyborgs sing – but Sirens have been regularly silenced in popular culture with the body's symbolizing of desire, not the voice. Siren thus transform into woman, into machines and most recently into sex dolls in the porn industry. If indeed one accepts this siren traversal from Greek myth, to technologies that emit siren sounds, to film, popular culture more generally, right through to the products of the porn industry – then the present book on Sirens might be of interest.

The mythical Sirens of Homer cannot be properly explained by recourse to merely shining a light onto the Sirens themselves; they are more properly understood in the context of their general role in Greek thought and in their subsequent adoption into Western thought to the present day. In doing so, it becomes necessary to focus upon who it is that constructs and listens to the Sirens and who gives them their meaning rather than on the Sirens themselves – who are after all – merely the construction of a Western male psyche. In following this line of reasoning Sirens become a product of male imagination – in effect, they tell us more about men than women despite the taking up of the mantle of Sirens by some women in the popular culture of the late nineteenth and twentieth centuries. This proposition is in turn problematic as it appears to silence the voices of Sirens in the very act of critiquing the nature of their origin. This conundrum is explored in the present volume as is the joining together of the mythical with the material in its sonic understanding of Sirens/sirens. It does so not merely to juxtapose them but rather to thread them together, 'tracing' connections, not as a unified whole, but rather 'prismatically' wherein the sonic is refracted through disparate historical and cultural examples to produce a range of 'soundways' defined by Rath as 'the paths, trajectories, transformations, mediations, practices and techniques – in short, the way – that people employ to interpret and express their attitudes and beliefs about sound' (Rath 2003: 2). These 'soundways' are expressed through a range of cultural 'traces' which operate in the intellectual and empirical shadows of Horkheimer and Adorno's *Dialectic of Enlightenment*. Few have ventured to join those sirens we hear in war and on our streets to those transformed from the written page to appearing on the musical stage of the world, in film, on the printed page and, of course, in social thought. Sloterdijk mentions this connection only to dismiss it out of hand.

> One of the typically self-revelations of the 20th century – and one of its most characteristic cynicisms – that it referred to the wailing machines on factory roofs, and in wartime also the alarm systems which spread panic in cities being attacked from the air, as 'sirens.' This choice of the name plays with the insight that sirens can trigger archaic feelings among those that hear them, but it distorts this with wicked irony by associating the siren

with a forced alarm. The most open form of listening was thus betrayed by terror, as if the subject were only close to its truth when running to save itself. At the same time, this renaming of the siren voice inappropriately coarsens it, instrumentalising it for the most brutal mass signals. Sirens of this kind are the bells for the industrial and World War age. They do not mark the sonosphere in which a joyful message could spread. Their sound carries the consensus that everything is hopeless to all ears that can be reached. (Sloterdijk 2011: 500)

Sloterdijk understands sirens within an anti-urban noise context while juxtaposing the destructive element of sirens to a romantic and reified projection of the song of the Sirens that ignores the masculine nature of its origin, and true to form, silences the voices of woman as representing anything other than their function in male desire. The present work prefers to ask what might a sonic dialectic of Enlightenment sound like? In doing so it uncovers the ideologies underlying the creation, presentation and understanding of siren sounds – as a dialectic of myth to materiality articulated through the criss-crossing of conceptual, cultural and empirical *traces* across time – of sound that entices, warns and destroys; from Homer to Hiroshima, from Kafka to Vonnegut, from Strabo to Kittler and from Walt Disney to Stormy Daniels – moving siren sounds from the cultural periphery to centre stage.

How then to deal with 3,000 years of siren thought, written about either centrally or peripherally in a multitude of disciplines – producing a Babel of siren sounds? The work eschews a linear approach to its subject matter in line with the playing with time and knowledge that lies at the heart of the siren myth. This book is written as a series of 'traces', loosely organized and after the introductory section to be read as desired, although the reader will detect some continuous yet refracted 'themes' in some of the entries.[5] The reader will not find a trace dedicated to the 'musical', the 'filmic' or to 'literature' but will rather find themes, examples and allusions cutting across disciplines. The book is a methodological homage to Ernst Bloch's *Traces* and Theodor Adorno's *Minima Moralia*, the traces as with Adorno's use of aphorisms are governed by their subject matter rather than any uniform length with the exception of the air-raid siren trace which given its exclusion from academic discourse is deserving of something longer. In the text of the book the reader will also note a recurrence – an obsession, with just a few lines from Odysseus's encounter with the Sirens[6]:

'The Sirens who sit in their meadow will seduce him
With piercing songs. Around them lie
great heaps of men, flesh rotting from their bones.'
'Use wax to plug your sailors' ears.'
'All those who pass this way hear honeyed song,
poured from our mouths. The music brings them joy.'
'We know everything the Greeks and Trojans
suffered in Troy, by god's will; and we know
whatever happens on earth.' (Homer 2017: 305–7)

These lines criss-cross through the traces as a bird in flight – arcing in the sky and settling on different branches. The Sirens, it is clear only sing to men and not to women. The ramifications of this simple observation vibrate, often unrecognized, through subsequent accounts and representations of the Sirens in producing an 'iconography of misogyny ... [that] still festers among us, kept alive by Hollywood and the world of advertising' (Dijkstra 1986: iv). The gendered nature of, and ramifications of, this confrontation weaves through the traces of the present volume. These are issues of knowledge, ideology, gender, sound and it's silencing embodied in accounts of the Sirens/sirens.

While Odysseus uses wax to block the ears of his sailors thereby rendering them deaf, the present volume, even though largely in agreement with Horkheimer and Adorno's understanding of the episode as representing the rise of the bourgeois individual and its concurrent cultural silencing of the oarsmen, focuses upon the multiple, broader social and cultural meanings attached to this 'silencing'. As noted – all women are barred from hearing the Siren song and in subsequent accounts the Sirens themselves suffer death for their failure to seduce Odysseus – how these multiple cultural silences play out is central to the present volume. But this silencing extends to the rationale and use of the sirens of war, contra Sloterdijk, an essential and embedded component in Homer's original account.

There is little physical description of the Sirens in Homer, merely that they possess lips, are able to sing and to sit. The history of Siren representation concerns the embodying of the Sirens as hybrid creatures who progressively come to represent all women in Western culture (Austern and Naroditskaya 2006). As the Sirens metamorphose, they move from land to colonize the sky, sea and the imagination. This cultural and physical movement of the Sirens is fully investigated in the present analysis as is the recognition that the Sirens are never 'seen' by Odysseus in the telling of the tale – the tale is a tale of the acousmatic – the sonic. The history of the Sirens is one in which they become progressively embodied suggesting, that in Western culture, historically, 'sound' is never enough.

The Sirens claim to have total knowledge and promise to sing to Odysseus of knowledge, past, present and future thereby overcoming time itself. This supposedly represents the power of their lure for Odysseus. This feature of the myth is central to Adorno and Horkheimer and features in the following traces as 'ideology' – after all the Sirens did not know that Odysseus had been forewarned of their charms and would survive – the seduction of sound fails, just as the following pages demonstrate that the warning sounds of sirens also often fail – but further than this – that, at least as far as the Sirens are concerned, the seductive nature of their sound also aims to destroy. The present short book cannot be a rewriting of Horkheimer's and Adorno's *Dialectic of Enlightenment*, its presence is but a casting shadow throughout the work, alluded to and questioned.

The above concerns constitute an obsessive circling around in the book as multiple traces of sirens are analysed, suggested and critiqued. The analysis is unapologetically cultural in focus and orientation and seeks to extend the parameters of what a sonic explanation of Siren sounds 'looks' like, or preferably 'sounds' like (Bull 2018).

The choice of which translation of the *Odyssey* to use was governed by two principles – topicality and clarity. There are over 100 translations of the *Odyssey* into English alone, yet only one – the most recent – has been translated by a woman, Emily Wilson. It is also a beautiful translation in verse. So that is the translation you will read in the following pages.

Siren Traces

1

Prolegomena to the Sirens

> [The Siren song awakens] hope and desire for a sublime beyond which, in fact is only a desert ... whence silence, like noise, burns all access to the song.
>
> MAURICE BLANCHOT

> The air raid sirens of Dresden howled mournfully ... Dresden was one big flame. The one flame ate everything organic, everything would burn.
>
> KURT VONNEGUT

Almost 3,000 years separate the episode from Homer's *Odyssey* in which the mythical hero, Odysseus is tempted by the song of the Sirens and Kurt Vonnegut's description of air-raid sirens sounding off before the destruction of Dresden in 1945. The Homeric Sirens fail to lure Odysseus to his death just as the Dresden sirens fail to protect the citizens of Dresden. In the Homeric tale there are no consequences to the failure of the Sirens – Odysseus sails on unharmed into the future and is written about and continually reinvented to the present day. In later accounts it is the Sirens who suffer from their 'failure', 'Upon hearing him, the Sirens threw themselves into the sea ... for they were fated to die whenever a man did not fall under their spell' (Jorge Luis Borges in Langer 2017: 145). The inhabitants of Dresden did not escape so easily with the deaths spiralling to anything between 30,000 and 115,000 on that night alone.[1] The Sirens of myth and the sirens of war are joined in name, cultural lineage and ideology.² Both siren accounts are 'side shows' to the main 'event'. The Siren episode in the *Odyssey*, a mere eighty lines from a 300-page book, plays a minor role in the narrative of Odysseus's successful journey home, while the Dresden sirens represent the state's largely impotent solution to the production of its own weapons of mass destruction in which there can be no 'innocents'. The sonic embrace of the Homeric Sirens seduce in order to destroy just as the sirens of Dresden, Hamburg, Tokyo, Coventry and Hiroshima are deceptive in their claims to protect in the very act of destruction; the one exclusive in its focus upon the listening male, the other, democratic in its annihilation of everything – animate and inanimate. Neither the Sirens of Homeric myth nor the sirens of Dresden are adequately explained by a mere reference to their 'sonic' qualities, rather requiring an understanding of the cultural matrix of power, ideology and knowledge in which they exist, are represented and experienced. Both Blanchot and Vonnegut place themselves in the shoes of the listener – the one 'desirous' for that which the Sirens signify; the other merely seeking shelter. One, a 'literary' reading from the page, the *Odyssey* is after all a book, the other thinking this is his last night on Earth – the one tempted, the other fearful. What of the sounds themselves? Blanchot, a literary theorist, knows the history of Sirens in novels and social thought recognizing that nobody has literally ever *heard* the Siren voice of myth, at least not until they became embodied in plays, operas and films like Disney's *The Little Princess*, where they become women. Originally 'the encounter takes place in the narrated imaginary itself', a product of what Don Ihde refers to as our 'auditory imagination' (Liska 89, Ihde 20017). In this cultural imaginary, the Sirens sing only to men, originally 'existing' on the margins of 'civilization', beyond sight. The history of their embodiment is a history of Western misogyny (Dijkstra 1986) and is primarily a story of men, not women. Vonnegut's air-raid sirens are 'real' but no less the product of a male-dominated culture, they are placed strategically, often out of sight – high up so that they might be heard. It is not the sirens that instil fear, but that which they represent. Vonnegut knew the destruction which modern warfare wreaks – from Guernica to Coventry, he listens to the destructive sounds of modern warfare whose origins lie beyond the sounds of the sirens – opaque in origin but direct in consequence. In this book, the Sirens of myth and the sirens of war play their role in a sonic renditioning of the *Dialectic of Enlightenment*. Adorno understood, as did Vonnegut, that the Siren myth extended beyond the literary imagination of Homer to be embedded in the core values of a Western culture from which the myth itself derived – these are the values of domination and instrumental rationality through which knowledge, gender, class and 'nature' are articulated, pursued and controlled.

2

Eclipsing the Acousmatic

The Story of the Sirens?

The acousmatic refers to a sound that we hear but cannot see or place. As I hear the distant sound of an aircraft in the sky, I might look up in search of it but might be unable to see it for a range of reasons, cloud cover, distance or poor eyesight. The situation is replicated countless times – a cry in the night, a creaking floorboard, the sound of a nearby automobile. Sonic experience invariably takes place within an embodied, multisensory and cultural context – even imaginary sounds or those sounds that are dreamt of in the middle of the night. Rick Altman in speaking of the relation of sound to image in film argued that 'sound will always carry with it the tension of the unknown until it is anchored in sight' (Altman 1980: 74). Can this observation concerning the sensory apprehension of film be extended more broadly to a wider range of sonic experience? David Le Breton thinks so: 'Every sound is associated with the object that gives rise to it, it is an object's sensible trace, a thread that connects us to the endless movement of the world that surrounds us' (Le Breton 2017: 65). Odysseus's encounter with the Sirens is acousmatic as he sails by he never sees them. He hears only their sound. Yet, the history of the Sirens is one of their embodiment in social thought and artistic practice. This history implies, in accordance with Altman, that *sound is never enough* experientially or conceptually. Nevertheless, there exist proponents of the acousmatic as a 'thing in itself' representing a conceptual, practical and perhaps ethical challenge for those who hold the view that '*sound is enough*'. Equally, however, for those who argue that the sonic always 'moves out' towards the visual, towards a wider phenomenology of sensory and cognitive experience – then the nature, value and choices involved in this extending of the sonic also require explanation and investigation.

The position taken in this book is that it is impossible to fully understand sirens sounds, both mythical and/or 'material' without recourse to the historical and broader cultural values within which they are experienced and created. Brian Kane, writing as a response to Pierre Schaeffer and Michel Chion's understanding of the 'acousmatic', argues that their position is one in which 'the acousmatic experience of sound allows a listener to attend to the sound itself, apart from the causes, sources and connections it might have to the environment' (Kane 2014: 5). Kane questions the philosophical desire or ability of a phenomenology of sound to achieve what Schaeffer and others hope to achieve whereby sounds 'speak for themselves' if only the listener possesses the requisite skills to decipher them. The abstracting of sound from its environment appears to deny its historic and cultural placement – its raison d'etre by rather locating its meaning in the ears of specialized listeners. Josh Epstein, in a similar vein to Kane, reinterprets Schaeffer's notion of acousmatic sound through the earlier work of the composer George Antheil whose aims appear similar to those of Schaeffer,

> The effort to produce a newly intense phenomenology of what Pierre Schaeffer later called 'reduced listening' – the hearing of sound without reference to its source, cause, or meaning – resembles Antheil's claim for *Ballet Mécanique's* purely formal intensification of sound. The problem is that nobody in the 1920s, excepting the purveyors of the doctrine, actually experienced Ballet Mécanique this way ... noise-music addressed the material presence of noise whilst claiming a nonrepresentational musical function. (Epstein 2014: xxiv)

Sound studies practice sometimes appears to fall into this category in which *some* examples of sound walks isolate, sounds to be heard rather than attempting to locate them within their cultural and individual context. Kane describes these acousmatic practices as 'a shared intersubjective practice attending to musical and non-musical sounds, a way of listening to the soundscape that is cultivated when the source of sounds is beyond the horizon of visibility, uncertain, undetermined, bracketed, or wilfully and imaginatively suspended' (Kane 2014: 7). In the following pages, it is not the inevitable contextualization of the sonic which is questioned, just as Odysseus might be imagined as craning his neck in the direction of the Siren sounds while tied to the mast of the ship as it moves beyond their singing, or as the urban dweller looks around for the origin of the police siren heard in the distance; it is that the turning of the neck in order to try to *see* is not a sufficient explanation in itself. The question remains, who is it that is listening and what is the cultural, historical or interpersonal context of their listening? A sound engineer working on the efficacy of police sirens will have a different sonic and perhaps ethical perspective from a worried middle-class listener, who on hearing the sirens feels safer due to her trust in the efficacy and honesty of the police, as against those who interpret police sirens as a potentially alien oppressive presence. Equally those who heard air-raid sirens heard them often 'acousmatically' but their meanings were filtered through their instructions to take cover – experientially this is how they are interpreted at any specific time or place. Warfare has developed its own versions of the acousmatic. From the First World War soldier poking his head above his trench in the mistaken belief that he would be able to duck on hearing a rifle shot to the belief that on looking up to the sky you would be able to see and run for cover from an intercontinental nuclear ballistic missile. Both the audio and the visual are enshrouded in their own cultural, political and ideological myths that extend beyond the siren sound, the rifle that fires its bullet, or the intercontinental missile flying towards its target – just as listening to the sounds of a disembodied Siren tells us very little.

Returning to the Homeric Sirens from where this book sets sail, we address a range of issues. To set the scene, Homer's original Siren passage is quoted at length, it is the page that has launched a thousand commentaries and over 100 English translations of the *Odyssey* from the Greek. The goddess Circe begins by warning Odysseus about the dangers that the Sirens pose as he embarks upon his journey home:

> First you will reach the Sirens, who bewitch
> all passers-by. If anyone goes near them

in ignorance, and listen to their voices,
That man will never travel home,
And never make his wife and children happy
to have him back with them again. The Sirens
who sit there in their meadow will seduce him
with piercing songs. Around them lie
great heaps of men, flesh rotting from their bones,
Their skin all shrivelled up. Use wax to plug
your sailors' ears as you row past, so they
are deaf to them. But if you wish to hear them,
Your men must fasten you to your ship's mast
by hand and foot, straight upright, with tight ropes. (Odyssey 2017: 302)

Odysseus is forewarned, what it is that is so beguiling and dangerous to Odysseus are the voices of the Sirens, they themselves are not described, only the site from which they sing, a meadow. Circe describes their song as deceitful, rather than consummation, death is the result. Five pages later Odysseus describes his encounter with the Sirens.

And when we were in earshot of the Sirens,
they knew our ship was near, and started singing.
Odysseus! Come here! You are well known
from many stories! Glory to the Greeks!
Now stop your ship and listen to our voices.
All those who pass this way hear honeyed song,
poured from our mouths. The music brings them joy,
and they go on their way with greater knowledge,
since we know everything the Greeks and Trojans
suffered in Troy, by gods' will; and we know
whatever happens anywhere on earth.'

Their song was so melodious, I longed
to listen more ...
But when we were well past them and I could
no longer hear the singing of the Sirens,
I nodded to my men, and they removed
the wax that I had used to plug their ears. (Odyssey 2018: 307)

In the *Odyssey*, Homer gives no description of the Sirens, other than that they have lips and sit while singing. They sing from dry land, not from the sky or the sea. It is unknown whether Homer meant for the temptation to be merely 'sonic' or whether the lack of description of the Sirens was deliberate. Yet, immediately after warning Odysseus of the invisible dangers of the Sirens, Circe describes the next danger he will face in graphic terms:

> There lives Scylla
> Howling and barking horribly, her voice
> Is puppylike, but she is dangerous;
> Even a god would be afraid of her.
> She has twelve dangling legs and six long necks
> With a gruesome head on each, and in each face
> Three rows of crowded teeth, pregnant with death.
> Her belly slumps inside the hollow cave;
> She keeps her heads above a yawning chasm ...
> No sailors ever pass that way unharmed. (Homer 2017: 304)

Scylla, like other female goddesses or women in the *Odyssey*, is described, only the Sirens remain 'invisible'. The reader, in this instance, must imagine their embodiment as well as the nature of the sonic enticement. Was the allurement one of pure voice, or the voice as a voice of nature, or of pleasure, or of the desire for total knowledge or, for an imagined body (Comay 2000)? Homer merely tells the reader that their song was 'melodious'; that they claimed to know 'whatever happens anywhere on the earth' and that their song was as 'honey – poured from their mouths' signifying the presence of more than one Siren. Commentators after Homer always referred to their physical attributes, their intentions and their placing. There is no abstracting of the sounds of the mythical Sirens – which of course began their life on paper as text, but may well have been spoken prior to this writing down.[1] The referencing of honey by Homer has also been subject to extensive commentary. Honey loomed large in ancient Greek culture as the only 'sweet' substance in their possession, not necessarily possessing the sexual connotations it was to assume in later interpretations. Catherine Liefferinge claims that reference to sweet honey in the *Odyssey* and in ancient Greece generally refers, 'etymologically ... to divine inspiration, while the poetic connection between sirens and bees, [refers to] animals with strong poetic and prophetic symbolism' (Liefferinge 2012: 1). If one accepts this viewpoint, it then supports the association of the

Sirens with knowledge and perhaps Odysseus's desire for that – whatever that claim might entail or constitute. The interpretation of the Siren encounter with Odysseus as merely 'acousmatic' has however held little historical appeal. Most interpretations merely assume that the encounter was an audiovisual one, with the use of the 'lips' as implying not merely a body, but a specific sort of body: Sirens become women in Heraclitus; birds that are part-women in Virgil; women metamorphosed in Ovid; and creatures that are half-fish half-woman in medieval and Victorian thought, literature and art. Historically Homer's Sirens, 'fleshed out', have captured the cultural imagination of successive Western generations in contrast to the more benign, ethereal yet physically identified Sirens of Plato's *Republic*. The range of Siren images in literature and art reflect the range of stereotypes, prejudices and roles that Sirens, as metamorphosed women, played in the psyche of male writers. The composer, writer and bishop, St Aldelm, writing in the sixth century was more tuned in to Western gender ideologies and stereotypes than Plato when he claims, 'Sirens are sea girls, who deceive sailors with the outstanding beauty of their appearance and the sweetness of their song, and are most like human beings from the head to the navel, with the body of a maiden, but have scaly fish tails, with which they always lurk in the sea' (Aldelm quoted in Lepfranc 29). This description contrasts with the ethereal Sirens of Plato who represent the sonic harmony of the universe which have failed to compete with the Homeric Sirens in the Western imagination, 'The Spindle turns on the knees of Necessity; and on the upper surface of each circle is a Siren, who goes round with them, hymning a single tone or note. The eight together form one harmony' (Plato 1944: 549). Equally, the ethereally disembodied sirens of Claude Debussy are a mere footnote to the representation of predatory Sirens in Western opera (Clement 1989). The representation of women in opera and the flourishing of the Victorian Siren in art and culture represents a perfect fit to the puritanical hypocrisy and misogyny of the period, 'sirens and mermaids were also an especially urgent problem facing the late nineteenth-century explorers of the soul. These daughters of the sea seemed to be virtually everywhere. Aggressive and predatory, driven by the ceaseless sexual hunger of the nymphomaniac' (Dijkstra 1986: 258) Siren movies of the 21st century continue this Victorian myth (see Siren 2010, Pirates of the Caribbean: The Curse of the Black Pearl (2003) amongst others).

In embodying the Sirens of myth, the choice of one form of Siren myth over another and its movement from the acousmatic 'voice' to 'body' represents a dominant cultural trajectory moving the placing of the Siren to the forefront of an 'iconography of misogyny' alive and well in contemporary writing and culture as Linda Austern and Inna Naroditskaya somewhat unreflectively claim, 'In western cultures, where the siren is most often seen as a dangerous seductive water-woman whose song envelops its listener in an open void, both space and the immaterial art of music have often been conceived as feminine. The woman musician becomes a siren, becomes sexually available' (Austern and Naroditskaya 2006: 4).

The history of the Sirens, from its beginning as an acousmatic encounter, has moved from the page as 'description' into the world of thought, imagination and creation as an embodied presence. These 'materializations' of Sirens require not merely a sonic explanation, but a sonic explanation that situates them within the culture which represents them and through which their meanings are refracted. At certain periods of history it appears that even their sonic presence, and hence any acousmatic presence, is denied in favour of the visualization of the Sirens. This point is not made to support what Jonathan Sterne refers to as an audiovisual litany but merely to chart the historical situating of sound, gender and vision in the history of the sirens.

3

Sonic Sleepwalkers

Siren Myths from Homer, to Bach, to Nancy Sinatra

Bach plays to God and himself in an empty Church.
WILFRED MELLORS

It starts in the water. In water that is deep and dark. Very low notes sustained for a very long time, then an arpeggio, then another; it wells up from the depths, it pushes higher and higher; the light, an indefinable light shines from above. And then it flows endlessly: 'The waves flow continually from right to left,' Louder and louder, the spring bubbles up its chords until …
A woman's voice rises. Then another, then a third. Even if you know nothing about them, you will guess (because they are underwater) that they are water sprites. Their songs follow the rising chords and accompany the water's flow. They play. They are fish-women who play in water. Their words are full of waves 'w's': their names are Woglinde, Wellgunde, and they sing liquid 'Weia's' and 'Wallal's'. It is all very

happy; these sprites, who are called the Rhine maidens or Nixies, have an explosive laughter. Women who laugh in water – the first image of the first origins. But, see what a funny father the Rhine is – a river!

(CLEMENT 1989: 139)

The myth of music as utopian sound is long dead. There is the sound, then there is the lyric and then the myth. This is not the place to reflect upon the potential overwhelming power of music, but rather to examine 'Siren' sounds. The weakness of Horkheimer's and Adorno's *Dialectic of Enlightenment* is that despite itself it still harbours a hope that even in the historic silencing of women there remains a utopian sonic trace, beyond damage – that lies beyond the myth of Enlightenment – yet this trace is itself part of a myth – despite itself – masculine. Judith Peraino sums up Adorno's position thus, 'for Adorno art music still harbours the mythic lure of the Sirens' song, which holds the key to resisting enlightenment as ideology' (Peraino: 2). The status of this 'message in a bottle' cast into the ocean is itself both forlorn and 'tainted'. Rebecca Comay repeats their error that a glimmer of hope remains in traces of the sonic past coupled with a disenchantment of the present articulated through the products of the culture industry, 'Who are the modern Sirens? If music's very essence is to be the "surviving message of despair from the shipwrecked", it is a sign of the times that it falls on deaf ears' (Comay 2000: 32). The view that in a world of instrumental rationality there exists only 'deaf ears' – commodified out of utopia – merely compounds the error that we should be looking to the voice, indeed a female voice, for redemption, for hope, for non-commodification.

We can imagine Odysseus strapped to his mast hearing the seductive sounds of the Sirens song that only he hears – a badge of his honour and place in the world as Peter Sloterdijk recognizes, yet Odysseus only survives the Sirens due to his status as the lover of Circe, who informs him how to outwit the Sirens – his fabled cunning merely a deceit:

> To hear them is to recognize that one's transformation into song is complete, and one's life goal thus attained … . Whoever hears

such songs of himself can assume that his own life is now a serious topic of conversation at the table of the Gods. This then is why the siren rock becomes the cliff on which the prematurely honored perish. There is no path leading back to everyday, unsung existence from the song grave in their own lifetime. (Sloterdijk 2011: 496)

The space between him and the Sirens is intimate – solitary, privatized – they sing only for him as his oarsmen, ears blocked with wax, merely row. The space is both expansive – open skies as far as the eyes can see and yet, claustrophobic, intense, engulfing and unsatisfactory. Odysseus sails on 'untouched', the 'beauty' of the Sirens song rendered powerless, whether their power of song be knowledge, 'we know whatever happens anywhere on earth,' or represents Odysseus's strategy of patriarchal control against 'the threatening power of female sexuality' as they sing their 'honeyed song, poured from [their] mouths' (Wellmer 2000: 6).

The Homeric Sirens are merely one version of this Western sonic myth. Instead of imagining Odysseus we might imagine, as does Wilfred Mellor, J. S. Bach playing the *Art of Fugue* in church, communing with God, also intimate – yet calm. As he plays, he listens to his own music as if it came from elsewhere – Bach stretching the symmetrical form of the fugue to its limit. Bach also wrote for female singers – his Mass in B Minor, written during the same period as the fugues – not commissioned, composed only for himself – untainted by commerce – in service to his 'god'. Goethe, on hearing the music of Bach exclaimed, 'It is as though eternal harmony were conversing with itself, as it may have happened in God's bosom shortly before He created the world'. Mellor's own reading of Bach, as Goethe's, is itself a historical interpretation entailing a set of assumptions concerning the mythical power of music. As does Richard Wagner's chromatic renditioning of the 'Sirens' arising from the depths of the Rhine; the one cerebral, the other sensual. Yet, in its sensuality Wagner draws upon a third myth – the origins of music as sexual violence as Alberich attempts rape against the Rhinemaidens in his opera Das Rhinegold. Three 'classical' Western sonic myths passed down through Western cultural history and all involving Sirens of some description, yet with only one claiming 'pride of place' as the dominant myth through which Siren sounds are understood, articulated and interiorized. The choices as to which version of the myth become materialized in culture are themselves of interest historically and epistemologically. Whether we understand Siren sounds as Homeric, symbolizing the enticing yet dangerous sounds of the 'female' voice, or as the non-sexual ethereal voices of cosmic harmony found in the writings of Plato and articulated in the music of Bach or as interpreting the Siren sound itself as the victim of male violence as in Ovid – they all are myths materialized through culture. It is ironic that the popular representation of Siren sounds as dangerous, as sounds only masquerading as enticing, is associated in Western culture with women/Sirens, whereas from Homer onwards violent sound is largely a product of male domination and destructiveness theorized so thoroughly by Adorno and Horkheimer in the *Dialectic of Enlightenment*. The inversion of who or what is sonically dangerous appears to join Homeric myth with that of Ovid in a sonic dialectic of Enlightenment. This dialectic was recognized as early as the fourteenth century when Dante 'twice represents the sirens as temptresses, and even makes the dream-siren of *Purgatorio XIX* mendaciously claim to have diverted Ulysses from his course, in *Paradisio* Dante considers only the beauty of their singing … but yet are no match for that of the heavenly trumpets which surpasses it as much as primary light surpasses reflected' (Lepfranc 28-9). The sonic battle between Sirens and the temptation of 'man' was articulated in *Jason and the Argonauts* some 2,000 years earlier:

> The men made ready to throw the ships cables to the shore, and would have done so, had not Thracian Orpheus, the son of Oiagros, taken up his Bistonian lyre in his hands and played a fast rendition of a quick rolling tune, so that its resounding echo would beat in their ears, thus blurring and confounding the other song. The lyre overpowered the virgin voices, and the ship was carried forward by the combined efforts of the Zephyr and the lapping waves which came from astern; the Sirens' song became quite unclear.

Orpheus' lyre thus becomes a jamming technology protecting Jason's men from temptation – disempowering the voice of the Sirens by the technology of man – yet as we discover below in Ovid's account of the origin of music – these musical instruments are themselves a product of male power articulated through sexual violence. But what then of the ethereal Platonic Siren myth – one of sonic symmetry, knowledge, peace?

The Dream of Seduction; Between Homer and Sartre

We are like sleepwalkers treading in a gutter, dreaming of our genitals rather than looking at our feet.

SARTRE

Sartre, in the above quote is referring to men – so is apt in relation to the present discussion of the Sirens of Homeric myth as representing the 'aural dangers' of the feminine. Austern and Naroditskaya (2006) in their survey of Siren songs point to what they interpret as a series of commonalities and differences in the cultural apprehension of Homeric Sirens. They point out that since their origin, 'they share an essential feature – their powerful voices – which render them desirable objects for poets, visual artists, and musicians to describe or emulate'. Moving on, they describe them as 'an embodiment of man's deepest fantasies, the Siren gives no sexual satisfaction without demanding his life in return' (Austern and Naroditskaya 2006: 8). The history of Homeric Sirens becomes the history of a Western 'male' imagination as articulated by Elizabeth Eva Leach:

> The siren's sonic lure leads ultimately to the dark, gendered underbelly of music's powerful effects, suggesting, in terms inherited from the ancient Greeks, like the Sirens themselves, that certain aural dangers are feminine and potentially feminizing. (Elizabeth Eva Leach 2006: 191)

The slide from aesthetics, embodied in the readings of the *Odyssey* to 'male' desire, is *the* dominant sonic trope of the song of the Sirens. Until the nineteenth century, the meanings and definitions attributed to Sirens were the exclusive domain of male writers, from Homer to Hans Christian Andersen. Austern and Naroditskaya correctly point to a shift in the latter stages of the nineteenth century whereby 'women came to re-claim her [the Siren] as their heritage. Women's re-appropriation of the male-created siren increased steadily throughout both centuries, perhaps as part of the global reclamation of femininity from male dominance and impersonation' (Austern and Naroditskaya 2006: 10). Thomasin La May and Robin Armstrong take this appropriation of the Siren extending it, problematically, to include all female singers, 'whether or not she wants the label, woman's singing in western culture has been inextricably linked to her sexualized body, a body whose ambition is to seduce, and this relationship is what can denote her as a siren' (Le May and Armstrong 2006: 319).[1] It has been but a short step to dispense with the Siren voice altogether when Annegret Fauser claims that Marilyn Monroe, hardly noted for her singing voice, was indeed a film Siren thereby further materializing the myth of seduction articulated in the body of 'woman' – whether she also sings or not. This embodying of the Siren as 'silent' woman predates Monroe and Hollywood. Marco Teodorski locates the silent transformation of the Siren to precisely that historical point when the attempted re-appropriation of the Siren is undertaken by women, 'Victorian Sirens stopped singing, the power of their voice shifting into their bodies. They became profoundly visual, epitomizing nineteenth-century scopic regimes of visual pleasure and voyeurism'. These images conformed to 'the prevailing male fantasies and fears of womanhood and of an unleashed sexuality' (Teodorski 2016: 46 and 200). Teodorski however overemphasizes the visualization of Sirens during this period by downplaying their role in literature, opera and the theatre of the period as is discussed below in relation to Wagner's representation of the Rhinemaidens in his Ring cycle.[2]

Harmonic Sirens

The myth begins with Plato, as we know he preferred metaphysics to empiricism. He also disliked the 'democracy' of the Greek Republic arguing that Greeks became the slaves of rhetoric. His solution was to advocate the training of leaders who would live separately from others, making decisions of state based on reason yet be unable to profit materially from their role. Plato received a poor political reputation for this heresy. Nevertheless, he was in one point alone more radical than Aristotle, our first empiricist insofar as Plato believed that being 'female' was no impediment to being trained to act as a guardian of the state unlike Aristotle who believed what his eyes taught him, thus supported slavery and the subjugation of women into domestic and sexual roles as merely empirically true (Nussbaum 2001). It is therefore no surprise that Plato reserves an elevated position for the role of Sirens in his myth of Er:

> The spindle turns on the knees of Necessity; and on the upper surfaces of each circle is a siren, who goes round with them, hymning a single tone or note. The eight together form one harmony; and roundabout, at equal intervals, there is another band, three in number, each sitting upon her throne: these are the Fates, daughters of Necessity, who are clothed in white robes and have chaplets on their heads, Lachesis and Clotho and Atrapos, who accompany with their voices the harmony of the sirens – Lachesis singing of the past, Clothos of the present, Atropos of the future. (Plato 1944: 549–50)

Plato's myth of Er influenced subsequent thinkers and theologians to see Sirens as being incorporated into a vision of 'music of the spheres' in which 'the entire world and all creatures in it[form] into one rational whole' (Leach 206). The medievalist Macrobius believed that the Siren referred to 'singing to God' and hence had an angelic presence. These beliefs fed into Christian neoplatonism and into the seventeenth-century science of Johannes Kepler:
'The heavenly motions are nothing but a continuous song for several voices (perceived by the intellect, not the ear); a music which ... progresses towards certain pre-designed, quasi six voiced clausuras, and thereby sets landmarks in the immeasurable flow of time' (in Kahn 2001: 245). These writers thereby affirm a divine character to music in which the Sirens either act to symbolize harmony or act as benevolent intermediaries for the living in their journey after death. Plato's Er also describes this alternative role for Sirens in the Gorgias. As Sloterdijk notes in this instance on post-Homeric Sirens, 'the Sirens normally performed a lament for the dead. Their power is borrowed from the underworld and its lords, Hady's and Phorcys; hence their voices are especially suitable for hymns of praise and songs for the dead. Their foreknowledge concerns human destinies and their unknown end' (Sloterdijk 2011: 495). This description resonates with existing funeral rites in many parts of the world where it is women who wail and perform laments for the dead. The musical lamenting for the dead takes on

a different meaning in our discussion of Ovid's tale of Pan and the nymph.

These Boots are Made for Walking: Sonic Myths from Ovid to Waco

The violence at the heart of Western music is articulated in the confrontation of Pan and Syrinx in Ovid's *Metamorphosis* quoted in full:

> Now Pan, wearing his pine needle crown, once saw Syrinx coming down from Mount Lycaeus and said to her – Mercury was about to repeat what it was Pan had said to her and to tell how the nymph spurned his entreaties and ran through untrodden ways till she came to the quiet waters of the sandy Ladon; how, since the river blocked her flight, she prayed to her sister nymphs in the stream to change her form; how Pan, just when he thought he had caught her, held marsh reeds in his hand instead of the nymph; how, as he sighed, his breath, moving through the reeds, made a high pure wailing sound; and how, charmed by this new instrument and the sweetness of its tone, the god had said, 'I shall always make this music with you'. And so, putting reeds of different lengths together, he fastened them with wax and thus preserved the girls name, 'Syrinx'. (Ovid 2001: 23)

Music in Ovid begins with the attempted rape of Syrinx. As she flees in fear, she metamorphoses into water reeds which Pan then cuts into pipes and he blows life into the 'hollow' reeds. So it is that Syrinx sings to the tune of man – as a passivized object. The objectification of the nymph as the sonic object of man is compounded in language with the term 'nymphomaniac' referring to a woman who possesses uncontrolled sexual desires, whereas in Ovid it is Pan who is sexually obsessed with the Syrinx, who in the tale, is a virgin. This male transference of sexual desire and attraction was given 'scientific' credibility in the nineteenth and twentieth centuries through the theories of Richard von Krafft-Ebing, Auguste Forel, Cesare Lomrosso, Gina Ferrero and others. 'Nymphomaniac' became a term that came to symbolize Victorian thinkers in their haste to stereotype women through the lens of their own masculine fears (Dijkstra 1986: 250). Ernst Bloch, usually such a perceptive cultural commentator, brushes over the sexual violence at the heart of the Ovid myth in referring to Ovid's tale as 'charming and allegorical':

> Playing [the Syrinx] gives Pan the consolation of a union with the nymph who has vanished yet not vanished, who remains in his hands as the sound of the flute. ... But gracefully and deeply though the need for music is indicated in this tale, it describes just as truly the small, momentous invention of music as *human expression*.

It is a contradictory-utopian goal: this pipe playing is the presence of the vanished; that which has passed beyond the *limit* is caught up again by this lament, captured in this consolation. The vanished nymph has remained behind as sound, she adorns and prepares herself within it, plays to need. 'The sound comes from a hollow space, is produced by the fecundating breeze and still remains in the hollow space which it causes to resound' (Bloch 1986: 1059–60).

Bloch understands the myth through the eyes of Pan with the subordination of Syrinx to Pan's desires – silent until he plays. Paradoxically, Clement, in her wonderful musical description of the beginnings of Wagner's Rhinegold with its evocation of music bubbling up from the water with the song of the Rhinemaidens, also downplays the violence of the scene, which is strange given that her treatise concerns violence towards females in opera,

> A rhythmic, heavy sound signals the appearance of the first man. He is a dwarf so ugly that the sprites tease him cruelly. They flirt with him, but he cannot catch them. He cannot catch a prey with a hand that can never grasp – this is important. The poor man can catch nothing by hand because the sprite's tails are slippery. (Clement 1989: 139)

The Rhinemaidens while having a minor role in Wagner's Ring set in motion the events that lead to the destruction of the world. The Rhinemaidens, like the Homeric Sirens, are outsiders, not thought well of by Wotan's wife Fricka because of their attraction to men from their 'watery lair'. Yet Wagner's Rhinemaidens, like Homer's

Sirens, possess 'superior' knowledge warning Siegfried as to his fate if he keeps the 'ring',

> Evil we know lies in store for you.
> To your own undoing you keep the ring!
> Just as you felled the dragon
> So you too shall fall
> This very day
> This fate we foretell
> If you don't hand over the ring to us.

While the Rhinemaidens possess superior knowledge, Clement focuses upon their role in tempting Alberich, Marie Euchner interprets the episode differently,

> Alberich refers to the nixies' hybridity, depending on his perceived relation to them: as long as he is hopeful that one of them will give in to his clumsy advances, he appeals to her human nature, only to dismiss her, as soon as he has been rejected, on grounds of her non-human fish-nature ... he then readies himself to inflict physical violence to force one of the three nixies into sexual submission. Deeply steeped in the belief that a man can get from a woman what he wants whenever he wants it, Alberich concludes:

> 'lusting, I languish after you/ and you must yield to me'. (Euchner 2012: 44) The seductive chromatism of the music itself acts as 'a sort of siren song that lures us to wallow in the operatic experience whilst forgetting the violence done to women'. (Smart 2000: 4)

But what of the point in Ovid that the woman/Syrinx only speaks through the breath of Pan (man)? We need to return to 1993 Waco, Texas, for a demonstration of this point. In 1993, the Branch Davidians had been under siege in their home for seven weeks after a violent confrontation with the Bureau of Alcohol, Tobacco and Firearms had resulted in deaths on both sides. In order to resolve the stalemate between both sides, the FBI had been called in to negotiate with the Branch Davidians. The details of the case are well known and was subject to a lengthy American Justice Department investigation after a conflagration in which most of the Davidians were killed, including many children. Of interest here is the use of sounds and music to intimidate the Davidians during the siege. Based upon prior experience the FBI blasted sounds through a loudspeaker system for twenty-four hours a day so as to demoralize the *Branch Davidians* into surrendering. These sounds included 'sirens, seagulls, bagpipes, crying babies, dying rabbits ... dental drills ... and a recording of a best forgotten Nancy Sinatra hit, "These Boots are Made for Walking"' (Reavis 1995: 260).[3] The use of sound and music as violent weapons has a long history (Ross 2016) but of interest here is the use, not just of industrial sirens, but the Nancy Sinatra song, 'These Boots are Made for Walking' whose lyrics go like this:

> You keep saying you got something for me
> Something you call love but confess
> You've been a 'messing' where you shouldn't 've been a 'messin'
> And now someone else is getting all your best
>
> These boots are made for walking
> And that's just what they'll do
> One of these days these boots are gonna to walk all over you.

The Davidians heard the threatening tones of Nancy Sinatra, not enticing to men and women alike, but rather threatening, yet in line with Homer's Sirens in predicting the future – these lyrics were sung by Nancy Sinatra, they were however written by a man – Lee Hazlewood to be sung by a man; the male threat articulated through the voice of the female singer, like a Syrinx transformed – the physical threat embodied in the song in tune with Siren ideology – a misogyny of control, threat and violence. The threat, at Waco, a masculine threat sung by a female voice. The sonic threat consummated as the Davidians were 'walked over' not by a female 'Siren' but by the armoured vehicles of the FBI Dick Schwein, the FBI 'negotiator' who had ordered the playing of 'torture' music against the Davidians said of the Davidians, 'No use trying to talk to these bastards. We've got to go in there and cut their balls off' (Noesner 2010: 89). Those without 'balls' suffered the same fate as those who possessed them as Waco was razed to the ground – a mirror image to the killing fields of Dresden some twenty eight years earlier.

4

Remembering the Forgotten Sounds of Air-Raid Sirens

Charlie Hebdo to Dresden and Beyond

> *One cannot dismiss the thought that the invention of the atomic bomb, which can obliterate hundreds of thousands of people literally in one blow, belongs to the same historical context as genocide.*
>
> ADORNO, CRITICAL MODEL: INTERVENTIONS AND CATCHWORDS, 2005

Air-raid sirens remain an uninterrogated part of the narrative of the twentieth century, of a confluence between the advances in technologies of destructiveness, the values underpinning these developments and the ideologies of protectiveness embodied in the use and development of the air-raid siren itself. The air-raid siren acts as a sonic sideshow to the destructive narrative of the twentieth century. Even in the act of listening, it is unclear as to whether it is the siren sounds that the city dwellers learn to interpret or the sonic trajectory of the aircraft and the missiles sent to destroy them.[1]

Air-raid sirens represent an ominous reminder of 'total war' and impending death from the sky; a truncating of space between the victim and the increasingly sophisticated technologies of death available. They are an ideology of sonic protection against the swiftly increasing threat of destruction visited upon subject populations in times of war. Sirens, in the main, are static constructions, as static as the subject populations who are to be attacked. This is in contrast with the increasing speed with which war is visited upon unsuspecting victims, from the 120 kilometres per hour of the Zeppelin attacks on London in 1915 to the 474 kilometres per hour of the B29 that dropped the first atomic bomb on Hiroshima to the trajectory of a contemporary intercontinental missile which flies out of the hemisphere at 1,000 kilometres above ground before it comes crashing down at 15,000 miles an hour, rendering sirens redundant and populations defenceless. As the speed and destructiveness of airborne weapons increase, the ability to escape destruction decreases.

Unlike the increase in power of airborne nuclear missiles, the sound and 'Fordist' delivery of air-raid sirens has remained largely unchanged until recently with their use in the cities of Mexico to Tel Aviv where they have transformed into smartphone apps, representing a twenty-first-century sonic privatization of warning. Their dominant presence in cities during the Second World War was continued into the Cold War world where they acted as dummy runs for the apocalypse and exist to the present day, in many European cities, in the Middle East, New Zealand, United States and Japan where they have morphed from warnings of a man-made apocalypse to those of the natural world – warning populations of earthquakes, tsunamis and typhoons.

Air-raid sirens represent sonic instruments of the state, re-inscribing the soundscapes of cities – placed throughout the city – high up on the roofs of buildings or on lamp posts so that all can ideally hear their subject populations become part of a 'collective' in their juggling of fear, hope and training. Air-raid sirens are equally a by-product of governments' attempts to command the air, the development of aviation itself and the ability to develop bombs and missiles that could attack and destroy cities from London to Hanoi. Sirens are the state's response to their own dialectic of enlightenment. They represent a Fordist technology, the muzac of human and latterly ecological destructiveness – primarily functioning and sounding the same wherever they are placed, and moreover evoking similar responses, despite any cultural differences represented by the cities and inhabitants of London, Coventry, Berlin, Dresden, Tokyo and Hiroshima.

While the sound and intensity of the air-raid siren itself has remained largely constant, that which it warns against has increased in power, speed and destructiveness. Just as the speed of destruction has accelerated, so space has shrunk both horizontally and vertically during the twentieth century. To understand air-raid sirens it is necessary to situate them within a complex and often contradictory cultural, technological and institutional matrix of the twentieth and twenty-first centuries. Sirens of war, as with Sirens of myth, are not to be understood in isolation. Air-raid-sirens are best understood as a response to the structural, political and technological abolition and transformation of space resulting in the negation of notions of safety zones associated with more traditional theatres of war. Air-raid sirens as distinct from the Sirens of myth have been largely absent in academic discourse. Sirens in their 'material' manifestation have normally been discussed in relation to the sirens we hear in our streets daily – those of the police, ambulance and fire services – or in terms of an urban aesthetic as they become incorporated into the sounds of the city as in the music of Edgard Varese or in their role as signifying conflict within city populations as in their use in hip-hop music. Whatever the reception of sirens might be – mythic or material – they are to be situated and understood in their historical and cultural context.

Sound in Historical and Cultural Context: The Sirens of Paris

While Paris is featured as a site of 'mythical' Sirens in twentieth-century literature, it is on the existence of material sirens that the present chapter focuses (Aragon 1999). This section begins with a personal recollection. It is 9 January 2015 at around lunchtime; I have just left the flat I'm staying in near the Cathedral of Notre-Dame in the Marais District of Paris. The normal noisy Parisian soundscape is transformed by the deafening two-tone sounds of police sirens which ubiquitously appear to be everywhere; above and beyond them is the eerie sound of air-raid sirens. These sirens are tested on the first Monday of each month in Paris – they exist to warn the inhabitants of Paris of terrorist attacks or impending natural disaster. But today is a Wednesday – although the time of day is the correct one for a siren trial. But then there are also the two-tone police sirens. The overarching air-raid sirens provide a blanket of sound into which the more localized police sirens provide ambiguous clues as to their placement.[2] The everyday sounds of the street are overlaid by the multiple sounds of sirens. Yet cars and buses continue their noisy path through the crowded streets. Those of us on the street, perhaps unconsciously caught in a time loop, look skywards – isn't this where danger is meant to come from? Some scan their smartphones for information, while others go into cafés to listen to radios or to make enquiries. None of us have been trained to respond to the sounds of air-raid sirens – to decipher their potential meaning and act upon them. Martin Daughtry, in his recent analysis of the sounds of the Iraq War, argued that 'a sounds salience and emotional charge depends upon the life histories of people who hear it, and upon the comparative backdrop against which they listen to the sounds that are emplaced in a particular time and location' (Daughtry 2015: 38). The sounds of the 'air-raid' sirens appear to be out of time and out of place in the bustle of Parisian daily life. I learn subsequently that the journalists of the satirical magazine *Charlie Hebdo* have been murdered by Islamic terrorists in another district of Paris – and were already dead by the time the sirens began.

In peacetime Paris, the concept of total war – of the indiscriminate killing of civilians – had returned – not with the sophisticated airborn weaponry developed from the First World War onwards, but with the discrete, traditional Kalashnikov. The localized brutality of killing was met with a public and global sonic warning system as the Parisian air was filled with the abstract sonic warnings of a country unknowingly at 'war'. Despite the continued use of air-raid sirens, Paris had not been heavily bombed in the Second World War and the Parisian experience of aerial bombing was limited. Parisians had feared being bombed in 1939 as the invading German army approached the city. Many had learnt, from media accounts of the recent bombing of Polish cities in the first months of the war and before that of the indiscriminate bombing of the Spanish town of Guernica in the Spanish Civil War a little earlier, what they might expect. The Parisian fear was that there would be no 'innocents' in the oncoming war – that nobody would be spared. While Parisians had been taught to retreat into their shelters with the sounding of the sirens, many had already taken evasive action by fleeing the city for the relative safety of Southern France before the arrival of German troops[3] (Drake 2015).

It wasn't until 1944 that Paris suffered aerial bombing and that was at the hands of the Allies, not the occupying German forces. Jean Guehenno, a Parisian teacher and member of the Resistance records, in his diary, the bombings that occurred on the outskirts of Paris:

> The air-raid sirens sounded for a long time this morning. After a few days of bad weather, the sky has grown very pure. The planes themselves were invisible, but we were surrounded by their noise, as a few of them – the fighter planes, no doubt were diving from a great altitude, thin white streaks would form and float forward, delicate as threads on a piece of cloth. The people were at their windows, rather happy to watch. ... We heard this evening that the military camps at Orly and Villacoublay were destroyed. (Guehenno 2014: 252)

Guehenno watched from a distance, as did his neighbours in relative safety, as if watching a film whereas those in close proximity were less 'aesthetically' orientated as one local worker commented, 'In the *Plaine St Dennis*, there were this morning 416 coffins. Several corpses remain under the rubble. An entire family, not far from our warehouse, met their end. Time bombs are still exploding' (Rosbottom 2015: 74). The soundscape of Paris was more generally transformed by the experience of war as was the reception of, and understanding of specific sounds conditioned by the experience of war and their occupation rather than from air-raid sirens. Paris, unlike the cities in Southern France, was an occupied zone. Sirens merely represented one aspect of a transformed soundscape which Parisians responded to from a variety of standpoints depending upon their roles within the city; whether they were members of the Resistance, a collaborator or merely a citizen just trying to survive in safety:

> Writers, such as Colette, emphasized how quiet Paris became during those years. Sometimes the silence brought benefits, when pleasant sounds – birdsong, music – were able to reach Parisians' ears. ... But mostly, the new silence in such a vital capital must

have been confusing and intermittently frightening. Police sirens were more menacing, airplane engines meant danger, a shout or scream demanded a more nervous response. The sirens must have been especially terrifying because those who usually sounded them, the French police, were no friends to the ordinary citizens of the city. (Rosbottom 2015: 105)

The politics and temporality of the Parisian soundscape described here is laid bare more starkly than in the Paris of 2015 experienced on the day of the *Charlie Hebdo* killings. Parisians, as in many other European cities during the war, were trained to respond to the sounding of air-raid sirens both on an organizational level and as civilians.

Air-Raid Sirens as the Last Line of Defence

Air-raid sirens represent the last line of a city's alertness, dependent on a wide range and continually changing set of technologies and social practices, sonic and otherwise, that support their use; from the tracking of radar and satellite facilities to the eyes and ears of lookouts who in the Second World War would telephone the potential arrival of the enemy after sightings. In Britain, for example, the Air Raid Precautions Act of 1937 created a system of localized wardens and air-raid posts which facilitated rescue in the advent of air attacks; and created a chain of radar stations placed primarily on the southern coasts of the UK, where aerial attacks were most likely to occur, and also at the outbreak of war facilitated the construction of domestic and public air-raid shelters:

> The radar chain was not perfect, and many of the crews operating the stations were not adequately trained. All the same, combined with the work of the Observer Corps ... and a well-functioning telephone system that drew all information together and fed it into Fighter Command Headquarters for processing and relaying to commanders of individual groups and sectors, the British defensive system was considerably more coordinated than the Germans believed. (Taylor 2015: 52)

UK space itself was divided into air-districts to monitor the movement of planes as they entered each sector. The movement of planes from one sector to another triggered off air-raid sirens as they entered each sector – either 'full alert' or 'preliminary alarms' to 'all clear' after the planes had left each relevant sector. Embedded in this sonic narrative was an inherent indeterminacy of effect – were the receivers of siren sounds to be victims or observers; were they targets or merely a staging post on the way to the destruction of others? This sonic indeterminacy led to feelings of both fear as well as nonchalance. The subject positions and skills and fears engendered by citizens who *thought* they were to be bombed, their responses and descriptions remained largely similar in the many accounts of bombing during the Second World War and beyond. This is not to be confused with the provisions available to populations in each city which varied across cities and nations. For example, provisions to escape any potential bombing in Tokyo, where only shallow uncovered holes had been dug by the population, differed from the Andersen shelters in the UK and the use of underground tube stations as refuges from bombing.[4]

Air-Raid Sirens and Sonic Doubt

While air-raid sirens had warned those in cities to seek shelter in air-raid shelters, bunkers, basements and tube stations with some success during the early parts of the Second World War in Europe, this became increasingly less so as the war continued and more cities were subjected to intense bombing. The scale of attacks also rendered the sounding of alarms problematic as wave after wave of bombers bombed cities such as Hamburg over a period of several days:

> In the confusion of the evening, the air raid alarms had been set off at 9. 30 p.m, followed by the all clear at 10, and then set off again at 12.33. The Hamburg police logged their 319th air raid alarm of the war at 12. 51 a.m. (Taylor 2015: 3)

The intended clarity of the air-raid signal was rendered increasingly problematic with the 'carpet-bombing' of cities like Dresden, Hamburg and Tokyo which destroyed the air-raid sirens themselves together with large swathes of the cities. As the war progressed, incendiary bombs were increasingly used as 'pound for pound' they created more devastation than normal explosives, spreading fire and destruction well beyond where they fell. This hyper-destructiveness was demonstrated in the bombing of Hamburg on 25 July 1945, when 800 US Flying Fortresses dropped a mixture of incendiary and explosive bombs on the city followed by hundreds of British bombers some hours later. The multiple sounds of the air-raid sirens and bombs in Hamburg were replaced with the sounds of a 'firestorm':

> Then the Hamburg citizens heard a shrill howling in the streets. The howling was something that had never before been recorded. The Germans named it Feursturm or firestorm. Within 15 minutes of the attack, most fires were blazing unchecked. As the fires linked and grew, they needed more and more air. Temperatures reached 1,400 degrees as the fire began to suck all the air out of the city. The firestorm spread over a 4-square mile rea and hit 16,000 apartment block frontages totalling 133 miles. ... Beneath these buildings were air raid shelters, where many people died either from heat or asphyxiation. (Taylor 2015: 7)

These scenes of devastation were replicated in many German and Japanese cities with air-raid sirens frequently giving confused warnings as wave after wave of bombers flew over – confusing both lookouts and radar systems, before the sirens themselves became silenced in the destruction.

> I will never forget this raid. I was in the city when it started. No alarm could be heard, because there were no more sirens. The chatter of machine guns and the howl of descending bombs told me unmistakably what was about to happen. (Later) I could hear a mobile siren (mounted on a car) sound the 'all clear' in the distance. (Knell 2003: 47–8)

The use of the atomic bomb in 1945 added immediacy to the mass killings of thousands in Hamburg, Dresden and elsewhere. Adorno frequently referred to the destruction wrought on Hiroshima by the dropping of the atomic bomb in his post-war writings. The sirens sounded when three planes, one of which was the Enola Gay, which carried the atomic bomb, were seen in the sky followed by the all-clear given moments before the blast that killed thousands of the inhabitants of Hiroshima in the blink of an eyelid. The sounding of the air-raid sirens would have made no difference either way. The power of the bomb rendering the air-raid siren redundant.

Sonic Training, Routinization and the Air-raid Siren

For most, the predominant experience of sirens was marked by the need to move swiftly; The hurried activity of waking and dressing (if sleeping), taking a suitcase and supplies to the cellar or running outside to a public shelter. A common experience was also that of waiting and listening in anticipation to determine whether an attack would occur. The sirens not only masked and even replaced other sounds in the urban environment, but were often accompanied by a silence due to the cessation of usual daily sounds.

— CAROLYN BIRDSALL, *Nazi Soundscapes*, 2012

In World War Two, the moment the bombs, incendiaries, and phosphorus canisters came down, the civilians were on their own. Ideally, but certainly not always, they had been warned by the sirens and had moved into air-raid shelter.

—HERMAN KNELL, *To Destroy a City*, 2003

Expecting the alarm was worse than the alarm itself, because at least during a raid one had something to do, bags to pack. 'I slept partly on my back so my right ear was completely free. Even in my sleep I always had a sense of listening.' ... One was in a constant state of anticipation, 'at the early warning signal my whole body was already trembling'.

—JÖRG FRIEDRICH, *The Fire*, 2006

Air-raid sirens demanded a training of the sensibilities. Responses to air-raid sirens were individual, collective and institutional – subject populations learnt how to listen, not just in order to interpret the meaning of the air-raid sirens, but also to listen for the sounds of aircraft and direction of exploding shells. City dwellers learnt how to wait, experiencing time in new ways – for example, they might estimate the length of time it would take to run to the nearest air-raid shelter. Daily life was reorganized with feelings of fear, expectation and resignation incorporated into the everyday. When Anna Freud questioned young London children during the London Blitz in the Second World War many said that it was the noise of the air-raid sirens that instilled fear into them – not the bombing; for adults it was frequently both.

Fear of death from the sky predated the use of air-raid sirens with the first bombings over London conducted by Zeppelins and Gotha bombers in 1915 and 1916. Subject populations had for the first time to train themselves to listen for impending death from the air. The experience of being bombed set the template for subsequent descriptions throughout the century. Maggie Turner, a nurse at Great Almond Street Hospital for children, describes the experience of being bombed in 1916:

> Never in my life will I forget last night. ... I fell asleep in a few moments only to wake up to hear the most awful noise ... [I] felt the whole of my room shake, things falling down all over the place, screams from nurses flying down the stairs and passages, saying quickly 'Nurses the Zeppelins are here!' ... The gas and the smell of the bombs exploding was awful, one after the other – the noise and darkness was too terrible. (Grayzel 2012: 40)

If the raid was a night-time raid – then listening was paramount. In the day, it was possible to look into the distance and still respond – but increasingly in the twentieth century, as the speed of flight increased – to wait in order to see was already to be too late:

> Danger was recognized by sounds. Once you could see something, it was too late to act. Shells and bombs were not visible, but they could be felt. People listened into the void to hear what was coming. When it was there, the sense of hearing was the first thing to shut down. (Friedrich 2006: 439–40)

Training civilians in the art of listening for the sounds of war was initially treated with scepticism by the British government in the First World War. This reticence among the political elite delayed the introduction of air-raid sirens at the time. The *Daily Telegraph* of the time reported on and supported the government position on not giving subject populations warning of impending attacks:

> The authorities say, in effect: 'If we raise the alarm all over the town when a Zeppelin is approaching, thousands of people will crowd into the streets, and if a bomb drops amongst them many hundreds will be killed and injured. These foolish people will not look after themselves by taking our advice to keep under cover, therefore we must protect them against themselves by not letting them know when the danger is approaching.' That, in very broad terms, is the line taken by those who are responsible for the safety of the public on the occasion of these attacks from the air. (Freidrich 2006: 236)

The UK government's resistance to the provisions of a public warning system in the event of an air raid was supported by employers who thought that alarms would disrupt the work process and make it more difficult to control their workers. After further air raids on London the mood of both government and the public changed, 'The Times reported that theatres, concert and music halls, and other places of "public assembly" would receive telephone warnings of future raids as early as possible, as would tramway authorities; rail and omnibus services would continue uninterrupted "for public safety and convenience"' (*Daily Telegraph*, 12 February 1916). While the British government was wary of the use of air-raid sirens in London in the First World War, there was no such reticence from the German government as they deployed sirens at their Zeppelin base in Nordholz. These sirens acted as both warnings of attack and as aids to landing the Zeppelin's in bad weather: 'Soon we heard the drone from the mighty engines of airships cruising above the blanket of mist. The sirens from the revolving shed and the gas plant howled their warnings up to the murky sky' (Marben 1931: 71).

Yet, as Birdsall and others have noted, despite extensive air-raid drills, training and the provision of air-raid shelters across the UK, Germany and elsewhere, when it came to being attacked the public response was by no means uniform – with the falling of bombs, individuals often lost their orientation due to fear and a sensory overload previously unimaginable among civilians. Yet even in the Second World War civilians frequently came to understand air-raid siren warnings as unreliable and hence paid little attention to them. For those cities that were under 'fly-paths' that were invariably taking bombers elsewhere to drop their deadly cargo – yet who were nevertheless subject to sonic warnings – a blasé attitude would be the frequent result. This blasé attitude towards sirens increased during the Cold War as sirens became both routinized and increasingly irrelevant to subject populations who often believed that the sonic warnings were merely 'drills', or that if 'real' would result in their destruction anyway. The sonic shock of war increasingly became a hypothetical shock maintained by propagandist messages and activities engendered by governments. When the Chicago White Sox baseball team won the 1959 American League pennant at a game in Cleveland, Chicago's fire commissioner authorized the ringing of bells and sounding of air-raid sirens in celebration. Two-thirds of Chicagoans – unsure of whether this was carnival or catastrophe – turned on their radios, the same number looked out onto the street, some discussed the situation with others, and a few phoned public agencies to find out what was going on. But among the half a million households within reach of the sirens, almost none (only 2 per cent) took protective action. Researchers concluded that even those who were frightened enough to want to take action did not do so because 'there is no action known to them that is worth taking' (Davis 2007:33).

Air-Raid Siren Ideologies

This country has been attacked by nuclear weapons. Stay in your fall out room until you are told it is safe to come out or you hear the "all clear" on the sirens.

(1992 BBC WARTIME BROADCASTING SERVICE SCRIPT.
NEVER AIRED)

As the Second World War progressed, the ability of air-raid sirens and other city defences to effectively protect subject populations diminished. Adorno defined the threat to human life in the epigraph of this chapter. Horkheimer and Adorno had famously defined Western progress in terms of destructiveness – from the slingshot to the atom bomb. Twenty years after this formulation, Adorno commented, at the height of student unrest in Germany in the 1960s that 'barricades are ridiculous against those who administer the bomb'. Adorno's position was taken, at the time, to represent an ethic of defeatism during the era of student protests in the 1960s. Adorno argued that the state apparatus which administered the atomic bomb was too powerful for the students to resist. While Adorno was discussing the effectiveness of 'barricades', the substitution of barricades with 'sirens' permits the development of a parallel proposition that implicates, not merely those who might wish to oppose state policy, but the state itself, which actively proceeds to produce an ideology of sonic hope for its subject populations. Yet, eschewing a simple either/or position, an historically and technologically nuanced analysis demonstrates that at times, like all good ideologies, they can be effective and at times serve to partially protect subject populations at specific periods of the ideology. Air-raid sirens themselves represent a shifting political, cultural, ethical and propagandist moment that differed in the early stages of the Second World War from the subsequent Cold War era. At the time when Adorno made the above comments there was widespread mistrust of any viable defence against the hydrogen bomb and even governments were scaling back on forms of civil defence. Nevertheless, American citizens remained subject to government campaigns to 'duck and cover' in the event of nuclear attack. The US government of the time had even trained a Ground Observer Corps to watch the sky for enemy bombers, this at the time of the widespread development of intercontinental ballistic missiles by both the US and Russian states. Because of this, sirens were routinely sounded in the United States both as forms of *sonic practice* and as *sonic warning*. The following American schoolboy recounts his typical monthly drill at school in the 1960s:

> We attended school at St Joseph, on the southwest corner of Willow and Palo Verde, and that was the very siren that sent us scuttling beneath our wood-grain-Formica-shielded desk each month – a desk apparently specially formulated to withstand the force of an atomic bomb.[5]

In the UK there was a national warning grid controlled by local police forces as police officer, Simon Neilson, rather quaintly recalls:

> Sirens were activated from a central point to give members of the public warning to take cover. In every Police Station front

office there was a small grey box on the wall with a receiver and small loudspeaker and on/off switch. When switched on it emitted a low peeping sound. The idea was that if there was an imminent threat of attack the device was turned on and if the beeping sound changed to a single humming note this meant you had a few minutes to take cover![6]

In parallel to creating a sonic defence network to be used in the event of a nuclear attack, the UK government took a range of measures to conceal the true nature of any impending nuclear attack from the public. It banned the film *The War Game* from British television sets for twenty years due to its dystopian and some would say realistic representation of atomic war, while nevertheless permitting the Hollywood blockbuster film of 1959 *On the Beach*, which showed the aftermath of a nuclear war as destroying all human life. The portrayal of the results of nuclear devastation differed dramatically in these two films however, with *The War Game* portraying brutally graphic scenes of devastation and government collapse in a manner that lay bare the absence of political discussion concerning atomic warfare at the time. *On the Beach* in contrast, while somewhat downbeat as a film, never showed close-up the physical disintegration and destruction wrought by atomic bombs. Showing instead fully intact cities devoid of humans who had been silently killed by radiation. The 1959 *New York Times* review of *On the Beach* pointed to the humanity of the film's portrayal of human extermination:

> Yet the basic theme of this drama and its major concern is life, the wondrous thing that man's own vast knowledge and ultimate folly seem about to destroy. And everything done by the characters, every thought they utter and move they make indicates their fervour, tenacity and courage in the face of doom.[7]

The UK government of the time had estimated that there would only be a four-minute warning for the arrival of any incoming intercontinental ballistic missiles, which would result in general devastation. A ten-megaton bomb, for example, was estimated to create complete devastation within a two to three square mile radius; making all housing uninhabitable for six square miles and with housing being set on fire for a fifteen-mile radius. A deadly radioactive fall-out would extend far beyond this area (Hennessy, 2011: 173).

Sirens nevertheless continued to be sounded around the world until the end of the Cold War in 1992 and beyond.

Persistent Sonic Ideologies

Today, air-raid sirens are used largely as warnings against natural disasters, or indeed have been decommissioned to be replaced by more precise and privatized sonic technologies that warn subjects. Sirens persist in Japan, Mexico, New Zealand and parts of the United States to warn inhabitants about potential natural disasters. They remain imprecise technologies, subject to false alarms as in the air-raid alarms in wartime. In Downers Grove, Chicago, the tornado sirens failed to go off during a tornado that hit the town despite the testing of the sirens each month. In Mexico City residents already complain of 'alert fatigue' as the 8,000 street sirens, meant to warn the residents of an impending earthquake, wail at the slightest tremor. The system of sirens had been installed after an earthquake in 1985 killed over 12,000 people in Mexico City. The earthquakes normally occur in the north of the country giving residents two minutes warning of a tremor. Meanwhile in Vietnam, the loudspeaker system installed during the Vietnam War in the 1960s and 1970s, once there to warn inhabitants of aerial attack, now delivers messages from local authorities, government and banks as a form of peacetime Orwellian sonic ubiquity delivered by the state.

While many cities around the world maintain a level of sonic presence through the periodic use and training of old air-raid sirens, the perceived threat of nuclear attack remains potent with the 'perceived' threat of attack by the North Korean state. In parallel to this are the tsunami and earthquake siren warning systems placed around the Pacific Rim. Public response to official 'ideology' is reminiscent of Cold War rhetoric and response. During the escalation of tension between the United States and North Korea in 2017, when North Korea sent test missiles over Japan, Hawaii started testing its own siren system as a result, placing 170 outdoor sirens on the island of O'ahu. The tests, carried out each month, consist of a fifty-second steady tone followed by a twenty-second break followed by a fifty-second wailing tone. During any actual attack

Hawaiians are told to listen for a three-minute siren signal and to tune into local radio or television channels to hear information and instructions. They are told to be prepared to stay inside for up to fourteen days. Hawaiians would be given twelve-minutes notice to respond to any nuclear missile launch, the warning time for Japan was less. When a non-nuclear test missile launched by North Korea flew over a part of Japan, the Japanese sirens wailed but again with mixed responses from many citizens, 'I was very surprised that it went over our area. This has never happened before. I was worried. Everyone felt the same. But what can you do? Hide? But where?' Another citizen pointed to the paradox of the siren warning, 'The alert told me to evacuate, but I couldn't think of any building that could withstand missiles inside town'. While the effectiveness of air-raid sirens in a nuclear world continue to pose problems of 'efficacy' for those who are subject to them, what then for tsunami warning sirens? The Pacific region is beset with tsunamis resulting in a large loss of life. Yet the response of authorities to the threat has been mixed. On the north coast of California, the state authorities considered that it was not worth the expense to maintain a siren system. The local fire chief stating: 'What do tourists do when they hear a siren? Without an intelligible voice message the siren is just noise'. Other researchers argue that 'warning systems are a bill of goods, a chimera. Warning systems have been greatly oversold by those who created them'. (Goldfinger. Director of Oregon's Univ Active Tectonics and Seafloor Mapping Lab). The danger of tsunamis is great however, in the Indonesian tsunami of 2004 where there was no sonic warning system around 250,000 people were killed. By 2010 a warning system had been installed, and when the tsunami hit the surfer island of Mentawai it arrived too quickly for most to respond. Also, remote areas were not covered by the warning system. As in wartime Germany, where bombing often destroyed the siren system, in Indonesia power failure after an earthquake meant that warning sirens remained silent. Intermittent warnings often mean that civilians do not know how to respond, whereas too frequent warnings produce their own form of sonic fatigue. In Mexico City after the devastating earthquake of 1991 a system of alarms were set up based on sensors monitoring seismic activity along the Pacific coastline. These sensors activate sirens when they pick up earth tremors of above five on the Richter Scale. Originally activated on radio broadcasts, the metro, schools and so on, now they are also activated on smartphone apps resulting in multiple 'false' warnings, 'When you hear an alarm you get scared because you know how loud it is, then nothing happens, and you are left unnecessarily panicked'. While some panic, others barely pay attention to the sirens, 'Whenever I hear the alert, I ignore it'. College student Gabriella Garay says that she prefers to respond to the slight tremors beneath her feet before she responds. Vibrations felt but not heard, personal experience, not ideology? (Gorbea 2015).

5

Urban Sirens

9/11, Dizzee Rascal and Varese

One can find a selection of 9/11 'siren clips' on YouTube – these are mainly audiovisual clips, the sirens mixed with a range of other sounds, some exclamations of shock, some people watching silently – horror-struck, others with indifference as some New Yorkers go their own way unperturbed. The overwhelming sound derives from a plethora of police, fire and ambulance sirens creating an intense Babel of sound – all sounds converging on the sometimes near, the sometimes distant Twin Towers. On some of the clips we see the first tower collapse in the distance – a mountain of dust rising high into the New York sky – so blue that the dust becomes starkly visible against it. As I watch these clips in the comfort of my study, I notice that the clips of siren sounds taken within the mountain of Twin Tower dust are muted, recessed, soft-grained much like the sound of sirens at sea in fog – their origin and distance unclear. This recognition is immediately replaced with a sense of unease – a sense of inappropriateness – what sirens sounded like under these conditions is, after all, not very important in the context of the cataclysmic occurrences of that morning.

On the morning of 9/11, 2001, I had arrived at university in the UK to see our departmental office staff glued to a small television screen, shocked by what they were watching. We all saw the second passenger jet turn and plough into the second Twin Tower – in silence. All of the images we saw were long-distance shots, silent and a little unreal. As the day wore on these silent images were supplemented by live on the ground reporting that gave greater presence – albeit mediated. It was only some months later on watching the Naudet brothers' documentary *9/11* that I and other viewers could watch an audiovisual account of the first passenger jet flying directly into the Twin Tower – engines screaming, loud and very fast. The Naudet brothers had been making a documentary about a 'rookie' New York fireman and on that morning the first call-out was to a suspected gas leak in Manhattan. With sirens blazing, the film crew accompanied the fire engine to an empty street where there appeared to be no gas leak. Just a normal false alarm filmed by the brothers. For after all the role of city firemen is a mixture of the mundane with the extreme. As they are filming we hear the roar of a very low flying aeroplane, not something one hears in Manhattan. The camera man instinctively looks up, attracted by the unusual noise and as the camera is raised, we see the jet plunge into the Twin Tower in the blink of an eye.

While the sound of emergency sirens is commonplace in New York and the subject of much debate concerning their use, loudness, inconvenience and frequency, in this instance there existed an unusual unity of purpose during 9/11. New York possesses civil defence sirens – air-raid sirens – these remained silent during the attacks on the World Trade Centre. In the short time span between the first and the second aircraft crashing into the Twin Towers – no one who controlled the sirens knew the nature of, or cause of the developing disaster – early reports mentioned a small private plane crashing into one of the towers – an unfortunate accident? New York, despite the rhetoric of its vulnerability to attack from the air, was not prepared organizationally or experientially. What would New Yorkers have made of the sounding of air-raid sirens?

My unease at analysing those audiovisual clips may well derive from the experience of analysing siren sounds within cities and my doubts concerning the veracity of such an endeavour. Sound travels through space, sound studies scholars understand vibrations and sounds. We hear or have heard police sirens, ambulance sirens, maybe even air-raid or tsunami warning sirens. Max Neuhaus has discussed the problems of locating the whereabouts of police sirens,

> It turns out these sounds have many problems, the major one being that they are almost impossible to locate. Universally people say that they cannot tell where a siren sound is coming

from until it is upon them. Unable to find the sound and becoming more nervous by its approach, many drivers simply stop and block traffic until they try to figure out what to do. Others ignore the sound until they are directly confronted by the vehicle, sometimes with lethal results. (Neuhaus 2003)

Siren sounds in themselves are not predicable or uniform in frequency, sometimes engulfing the space with sound, creating a sonic surge or swarm as in Manhattan in 2004, 'as many as 80 police cars quickly stream out of nowhere, in neat rows, their lights and sirens going. The drills seem to take place on blocks with restricted parking, and each car executes a fast back-in parking job against the curb' (Wilson 2004). On this occasion the New York police were practising for the Republican Convention of that year to be held in New York but it left the public who experienced this 'swarm' nonplussed. While New Yorkers might well come together to support the sirens of 9/11 their continued loud and abrasive presence has garnered recent opposition that may spell the end of the sirens in their present form. Those who live nearby police stations, fire stations and hospitals often complain of being unable to sleep, resulting in the New York authorities considering a move towards a more European two-tone siren. Some question the need to use sirens at all in the majority of cases, especially at times when there is little or no traffic on the streets. Noise abatement societies are alive and well in New York (Aratani 2019).

The architectural layout of cities together with the technologies that are habitually used – hermetically sealed motor cars containing wrap-around sound systems, headphones as accompaniments to the walking of the city and so on – affect people's ability to hear or apprehend sound, resulting in an increased use of visual warning signs acting as an accompaniment to the sonic warning of sirens. American cities do not keep records on how many times sirens might sound in New York, Washington or Los Angeles. Collating them with the number of emergency calls is inaccurate as those who respond to calls do not always turn on their sirens. The common use of sirens is generally accepted though. Van Lengen on interviewing a member of the Los Angeles Fire Department, responsible for an urban sprawl of 469 square miles was informed that, 'we have roughly 1,277 incidents per day and probably go to at least 100 of those without lights and sirens, but that's an aggressive guess.

So I would be comfortable saying we responded at least 400,000 times last year with sirens' (Van Lengen 2016: 3). Responses to the actual sound of sirens varies according to who is engaging in the listening – whether they hear sirens as salvation or threat – but also in terms of any general noise abatement concerns. It is also an issue of geography. The experience of many inhabitants of Washington, for example, is that siren sounds are more disruptive than those of New York – a city which has a greater intensity of siren use. In response to this varied response to siren sounds, Van Lengen points to the different physical layout of both cities:

> If you compare DC to New York you'll find in Manhattan a much more acoustically alive environment than Washington, where you have wide open avenues, you have boulevards, you have open space in a way that New York just does not have. In New York, with its millions of people packed into a relatively small space, the sound of the city has nowhere to go because the buildings are so high and because they create these kind of canyons of space, the sound doesn't go away – it reverberates against the facades all the way up. So it's actually a much noisier city that Washington. (Van Lengen: 4)

It was in 2009, some eight years after 9/11, that British sound artist Paul Elliman took a group of sound scholars through the nocturnal streets of New York in order to listen to the city's sirens – police, fire and ambulance. The participants were armed with the New York codes for the use of a variety of siren sounds to be used dependent on the situation. The aim of the event was to listen to and understand siren sounds – the assumption being that sirens 'represent an apparently unambiguous message of stress, alarm, or danger within the city'. The group of sound scholars were well educated, young and predominantly white. The group unfortunately heard few sirens on their walk. They were informed that they had gone to the 'wrong' area of New York. Those areas with higher crime rates, they were reliably informed, such as the South Bronx or Brownville had more siren sounds. The scholars had walked from Cooper Square between the Bronx and Greenwich Village, wealthier areas of the city, where else would young sound scholars go? The image – it is recorded on film – of sound scholars walking around the 'wrong' area of New York in order to understand the nature and meaning of urban sirens is troubling on many levels, as indeed is going to the 'correct' areas of a city in an attempt to describe siren sounds. It represents sonic voyeurism masked as investigation. Leaving aside the issue concerning the aims and purposes of urban sound walks in general, this example illustrates that a phenomenology of listening needs to take into account the social, political, historical and economic nature of those sounds listened to together with a critical reflection on the nature of those who are engaged in 'listening' (Bull 2018). British police officers in Essex also displayed a failure to understand the cultural specificities of New York police sirens when two members of Chelmsford's police force, while bored, on night duty blasted out 'Sound of Da Police', a rap song whose chorus goes, 'Woop, woop, it's the sound of da police'. The songs performers, *KRS-One* evoked the sound of police sirens in the Bronx. In order to understand the sectional and conflicting nature of urban siren sounds from New York to London we turn to the UK rapper, Dizzee Rascal:

> I can hear the sirens coming
> Better run when you hear the sirens coming.
>
> Dizzee Rascal 2006

Equally, Masta Ace's *Jeep Ass Niguh* (1993) featuring police sirens as the subject of their song as the protagonist gets pulled over for making his own form of New York public noise singing, 'rolling down my windows, yea, I have an air conditioner/But I got the sound I want the whole world to listen ta'. Subject populations in American cities and elsewhere experience the sound of police sirens differently as is well documented, from the recent rise of the Black Lives Matter movement to the depressingly consistent figures of black lives lost at the hands of the American police force (31 per cent of police killings from 13 per cent of the population and 63 per cent of those killed when they were unarmed) or, indeed, the disproportionate percentage of black citizens in jail (Washington Post 2019).

Sounds as we have learnt from Mark Smith's pioneering work on Antebellum America are sectionally heard with the racialization of 'listening' in the United States provocatively demonstrated most recently in the work of Jennie Stoever. Karin Bijsterveld and others have also charted the historical opposition to a range of urban sounds through analysing anti-noise societies active throughout the twentieth century. Sound studies has had greater success in its understanding and analysis of the functioning of urban sirens as mere acts of hearing than in the social contextualization of those sounds as carried out in the present book.

Sirens and Nostalgia

Historically, factory sirens have punctuated the daily lives of workers – sounding at the start and end of lunchtime to tell workers it was either time to leave or go back to work. For many this would represent a five- to ten-minute trip to the factory. This was a time when the workforce lived locally and could hear the factory sirens. Each mill would have its own siren sound, just as in Alain Corbin's analysis of rural French church bells – each would have its own timbre and could be heard throughout each parish. In Bangor, Wisconsin, there was a long tradition in maintaining the old factory sirens: 'At noon, a sudden siren broke the cold silence in this small town. It wailed for 10 seconds, then fell to a low, long purr.' The Hussa Brewery from which the siren had been taken had closed many years earlier, but the siren remained sounding daily at 7.00 am, noon, 6.00 pm and 10.00 pm. The siren caused some discord, with some finding it a nuisance while others found it comforting – reminding them of a link to their town's past, rather as we might linger over an old record sleeve from our youth. The town council had agreed to turn off the sirens for a trial ninety-day period in order to gauge the local response but stopped the trial after a few days due to local protests. Sonic nostalgia had won for now. 'In the local town bar, "Butchie" Hansen 79, drank La Crosse Lager in a can cooler kept for him behind the bar. He moved to Bangor in 1984 and relies on the 7 am whistle as an alarm clock. "The noon whistle", another man said, "reminds him it's time for lunch". And at this bar, the 6.00 pm siren signals the end of happy hour' (Ross 2015).

Urban sirens and the study of sound need not restrict itself to the vicissitudes of warning and salvation or regulation. As we have noted in the music of Dizzee Rascal – sometimes these concerns are expressed as song or entertainment as with the plethora of songs, often hip-hop, that use the actual sounds of sirens as part of, or as a motif to describe the experience of living in the city.

Beyond this lies one of the foundational moments of sound studies itself which questions the very relationship between sound, for some noise, and music. The association of sirens to urban sound became an important tenet of early-twentieth-century music making – an aestheticization – but an aestheticization embodying a range of differing material ideologies. Foremost among these was the work of the Russian revolutionary composer Arseny Avraamov who in 1922 performed his 'Symphony of Factory Sirens' in Baku in order to celebrate the fifth anniversary of the October Revolution in Russia. The symphony, not recorded, used a wide variety of sirens together with a renditioning of the Internationale and Marseillaise sung by choirs and the public. Avraamov rejected any distinction between performers and listeners, expecting everybody to play a part either singing or in making other industrial noises. Importantly, Avraamov did not consider his performances as avant-garde in the European tradition. Indeed, he thought the twelve-tone system of music developed by Arnold Schoenberg and others irredeemably decadent and bourgeois. For the performance of the Symphony of Sirens,

> Avraamov worked with choirs thousands strong, foghorns from the entire Caspian flotilla, two artillery batteries, several full infantry regiments, hydroplanes, twenty five steam locomotives and whistles and all the factory sirens in the city. He also invented a number of portable devices, which he called steam whistle machines for this event, consisting of an ensemble of 20 to 25 sirens tuned to the notes of the The Internationale. He conducted the symphony himself from a specially built tower, using signalling flags. ... Avraamov did not want spectators, but intended the active participation of everybody in the development of the work through their exclamations and singing, all united with the same revolutionary will. (Smirnov 2013: 29)

Avraamov himself pursued a self-conscious course of social and economic liberation which he perceived embodied all Russians since the October Revolution, in this ideology sirens were seen as an ideal replacement for church bells in the Russia of the 1920s as church bells were seen as bourgeois as against the industrial and proletarian sound of sirens.

At around the same time, but in New York, the émigré French composer Edgard Varese was composing his *Ameriques* for a large classical orchestra with the additions of siren and steamboat whistles. Varese's music, unlike Avraamov's, was labelled 'avant-garde' and was destined for the classical concert hall rather than the city street. Its first performance was conducted by Leopold Stokowski with the Philadelphia Orchestra and took place in New York's Carnegie Hall. While Dvorak's New World Symphony, also written by a European composer, but in 1893 (but also premiered at Carnegie Hall) conjures up images of vast open spaces and reflects on a rich cultural mix of musical sources, Varese's *Ameriques* appears fully 'urban' much like the music of Dizzee Rascal. Varese describes composing in his New York apartment,

> For the first time, with my physical ears I heard a sound that kept recurring in my dreams as a boy – a high whistling C – sharp. It came to me as I worked in my westside apartment, where I could hear the river sounds – the lonely foghorns, the shrill peremptory whistles – the whole wonderful river symphony which moved me more than anything ever had before. (in Huscher 1995)

We are not sure what the audience/performers thought of Avraamov's Symphony of Sirens but the New York performance of *Ameriques* produced a level of scorn and ridicule from its audience and critics alike with one critic citing Varese's use of a siren as 'a symphonic genuflection to the Fire Department and the Pneumatic Riveter's Union' (Huscher 1995).

Sirens for the masses and sirens for the elite, the place of performance and the cultural and ideological context of the aesthetics of the urban siren filters through the composition, performance and reception of the sonic just as the everyday sound of the police siren invokes a range of responses based upon the social positioning of the listener. Sirens do not speak for themselves.

6

Timing the Sirens

Kurt Vonnegut Meets Theodor Adorno

Homer's Sirens subvert time in their song to Odysseus. The promise attached to this subversion is death. If Homer were writing today, he would probably write science fiction. Homer writes:

> The music brings them joy,
> And they go on their way with greater knowledge,
> Since we know everything the Greeks and Trojans
> Suffered in Troy, by gods' will; and we know
> Whatever happens anywhere on earth.

The song, like their promise, is flawed for if they knew the future then they would have known that Odysseus sails on unable to succumb to their sonic temptation, whether this be song or promise (Pucci 1998: 7). So perhaps, as Odysseus sails on he recognizes the fallibility of their knowledge – the song unsung, the promise incomplete. Other than defeating the Sirens and living to fight another day in his quest to return home, the episode's resonance remains in Western cultural discourse if not, paradoxically, in the *Odyssey* itself where the theme disappears. After all, the Sirens in Homer were not that big a deal – a few lines after all. The interesting story is what comes after Homer after all.

Kurt Vonnegut emerges as a twentieth-century Homer in his subversion of time in his 1955 'science-fiction' novels *The Sirens of Titan* and *Slaughterhouse 5* from 1968. *Slaughterhouse 5* alludes to the mass destruction of Dresden by British bomber command in 1945, an event experienced by Vonnegut as a young American prisoner of war. Vonnegut, like many victims of war, felt unable to write about his experience until some years later – as it turned out during the Vietnam War so publicly aired on American television. Vonnegut later comments that 'of course, another reason not to talk about war is that it's unspeakable' (Vonnegut 2006). Apart, maybe, as science fiction, which is not after all, lyric poetry which Adorno stated was impossible after Auschwitz. However, the readers of Vonnegut did not need to wait until 1968 for a fictional renditioning of war as this exists in his earlier novel – *The Sirens of Titan* – both novels play with time, war, prophecy and, importantly, sirens. Vonnegut remains the only novelist in which the mythical Sirens of Homer and the air-raid sirens of war co-exist 'out of time'. They both create an imaginary pallet deriving from the trauma of his wartime experience with Vonnegut commenting that his overall work, 'is about the inhumanity of many men's inventions to man. This is the dominant theme of what I have written during the last forty-five years or so' (in Beidler VolXLIX, issue 1, 2010: 8).

The sirens in *Slaughterhouse 5* act as a sideshow to the main theme of the book as they do more generally in war. Vonnegut lives below ground with other POWs in a Dresden abattoir – where animals are killed for human consumption – ironically it is this killing room that saves him on the night of the bombing. Accounts of the night of 13 February 1945 in Dresden point to a city at peace, when the air-raid sirens sounded at 9.51 pm people were returning home from Shrove Tuesday celebrations.

> The city had no air defences as these had been moved elsewhere to protect the industrial areas of Germany. Ten minutes after the air-raid sirens began their wailing, flares lit up the Dresden sky with around eight hundred Avro Lancaster bombers dropping 1,400 tons of high explosion and 1,180 tons of incendiary bombs onto the defenceless city. The intensity of the firestorm created superhot tornadoes, mile high vortexes ripping oxygen from the air to feed their roaring thermal engines. (Taylor 2004: 78)

Vonnegut thought that 135,000 people were killed that night.

Vonnegut had every reason to subvert time and both *The Sirens of Titan* and *Slaughterhouse 5* play with time through their main character's engagement with a fictitious planet named Tralfamadore, which plays a central role in both novels – the one supposedly about mythical sirens, the other concerning the real destruction that air-raid sirens warn of. Billy, an ophthalmologist by trade, the main character of *Slaughterhouse 5*, remains traumatized by his experiences at Dresden and copes with the trauma by 'imagining' himself as the victim of an alien abduction from the planet Tralfamadore, which possesses a dramatically different sense of time to that of Earth. One in which he moves effortlessly into the past and into the future and where he learns that nothing about time is changeable – that there is no free will:

> Billy has gone to sleep a senile widower and awakened on his wedding day. He has walked through a door in 1955 and come out another one in 1941. He has gone back through the door to find himself in 1963. He has seen his birth and death many times, he says, and pays random visits to all events in between. (Vonnegut 2019: 19)

> The most important thing I learned on Tralfamadore was that when a person dies he only *appears* to die. He is still very much alive in the past. ... All moments, past, present, and future, always have existed, always will exist. ... They can see how permanent all the moments are, and they can look at any moment that interests them. It's just an illusion we have here on Earth that one moment follows another. ... When a Tralfamadorian sees a corpse, all he thinks is that the dead person is in bad condition in that particular moment, but that the same person is just fine in plenty of other moments. (Vonnegut 2019: 22)

In the act of rejecting the trauma of his wartime experiences Billy creates an alternative sense of time in which all experience is understood simultaneously and randomly. Billy becomes a twentieth-century Siren – not a woman, and he doesn't sing. On telling others of his newfound knowledge, Billy is restrained – tied up – not like Odysseus voluntarily, and is placed in a hospital for the mentally ill. As sound continues to exist – out of time – in memory and traumatized flesh so Vonnegut represents this, more literally, on hearing a siren sound in peacetime America: 'A siren went off, scared the hell out of him. He was expecting World War Three at any time. The siren was simply announcing high noon. It was housed in a cupola atop a firehouse across the street from Billy's office. Billy closed his eyes. When he opened them, he was back in World War Two again' (Vonnegut 2019: 48–9).

In Vonnegut's *The Sirens of Titan* the Sirens appear as in the myths of Greek culture and not those of war – although war is a central theme of the novel. Central to the plot is the character of Constant Rumfoord who plays a dual role, that of prophet of the future – another male Siren, and as orchestrator of war between Mars and Earth in which he knows that Mars will lose thereby permitting him to create his own messianic religion on Earth, the Church of God the Utterly Indifferent. Rumfoord and his dog Kazak are space travellers who have disintegrated into wave phenomena only to materialize on Earth for one hour every forty-seven days in order to tell people on Earth what the future holds and, by extension, what has existed in the past, 'When I ran my spaceship into the chrono-synclastic infundibulum, it came to me in a flash that everything that has ever been will be, and everything that ever will be has always been' (Vonnegut 1999: 20).

'Chrono' means time in the novel, and 'synclastic' refers to time curved towards the same side in all directions and 'infundibulum' means a funnel and shares conceptual traces with Plato's myth of Er in the *Republic*. In the novel, unlike in Homer's *Odyssey*, Vonnegut describes people as unwilling to hear about their individual destinies. Central to the novel is the character of Malachi, a rich playboy who Rumfoord informs that he will marry Rumfoord's own wife and have a child on the planet Titan, and that he, Rumfoord has already met him there. In the scene, Malachi shows Rumfoord a photo of his beautiful girlfriend – Miss Canal Zone – and in response, Rumfoord shows him a photograph of three Sirens whose 'beauty was to the beauty of Miss Canal Zone as the glory of the Sun was to the glory of a lightening bug'. This is the first of only four times that the Sirens are mentioned in the novel – a sideshow but simultaneously central. Malachi takes the photograph and the next time Rumfoord sees the Siren image it is as a magazine image advertising cigarettes. The caption states:

Pleasure in Depth! said the headline on the ad. The picture that went with it was the picture of the three Sirens of Titan.

They were – the white girl, the golden girl, and the brown girl. The fingers of the golden girl were fortuitously spread as they rested on her left breast, permitting the artist to paint in a Moonlight Mist Cigarette between two of them. The smoke from her cigarette passed beneath the nostrils of the brown and white girls, and their space-annihilating concupiscence seemed centred on mentholated smoke alone. Rumfoord had known that Constant would try to debase the picture by using it in commerce. (Vonnegut 1999: 40–41)

Vonnegut separates the visual allure of the Sirens from their voicing of the prophetic. In doing so he represents the Sirens *as image* – they are, it transpires, photographs of painted statues on the planet Titan, constructed by Salo, a shipwrecked spaceman from Tralfamadore – the images concern the nature of male desire rather than the Sirens themselves. The prophetic nature of the Siren song becomes no song at all, yet its power over the male psyche reigns supreme. This becomes apparent later in the novel where Malachi who has been kidnapped along with thousands of others and sent to Mars 'where their memories were wiped and controlled by antennas placed in their skulls' by Rumfoord in order that they might wage war unknowingly against Earth, faintly remembers only one image, the vision of the three Sirens, 'There were three beautiful women in that paradise, and Malachi knew exactly what they looked like. ... He even remembered the brand of the cigarette the golden girl was smoking, "Sell Moonmist"' (Vonnegut 1999: 78).

In the event, all of Earth's activities were merely unknown signals made between the Tralfamadorians and their lost spaceman in an effort to rescue him, 'World monuments were merely messages sent by the Tralfamador's telling Salo help was on its way! Stonehenge when viewed from above says, "Replacement part being rushed with all possible speed"' (Vonnegut 1999: 191).

It transpires that Salo's journey was not to Earth at all but to a more distant galaxy, he had merely landed in Earth's galaxy due to a fault on his ship, 'Everything that the earthlings had ever done has been warped by creatures on a planet one-hundred and fifty thousand light years away' (Vonnegut 1999: 207). The novel ends with an old and disillusioned Rumfoord tending his dilapidated swimming pool on Titan, the three Sirens remaining at the bottom of the pool. He looks at them indifferently, 'they didn't mean much to him now, really, except to remind him that sex had once bothered him' (Vonnegut 1999: 217).

If Horkheimer and Adorno's *Dialectic of Enlightenment* is read as myth-producing forms of destructiveness masquerading as rationality, then Vonnegut provides us with a science-fiction version of their thesis. Vonnegut dismantles the Enlightenment myth through alternative means. For him, the myth of Enlightenment rationality is located in the unknown actions of another people from an 'unknown' planet made for different purposes. The mythical Sirens of Homer become associated with the figures on Greek vases reconstructed as 'exotic', yet merely inanimate three-dimensional statues, silently reproduced as photographs – the desiring male image commodified as cigarette advertisements which produce their own form of desire and death. Vonnegut continues with an Adornian image of the cultures of commodification in *Slaughterhouse 5* making a direct comparison between the bombing of Dresden and Billy's redeveloped home town,

> Billy drove through a scene of even greater desolation. It looked like Dresden after it was fire bombed – like the surface of the moon. The house where Billy had grown up was so empty now. This was urban renewal. (Vonnegut 2019: 49)

This is the logic of the Enlightenment rationality, not merely in the commodified image of the Siren but in the timeless fabric and make up of daily life. There is no evidence that Vonnegut ever read Adorno or, for that matter, that Adorno had ever read Vonnegut – for after all – it was as if Vonnegut had come from a different planet.

7

Siren Spaces

A Different Colonization?

> To arrive there means death, and the luring song of the
> Sirens is the call coming from the void.
>
> (LISKA 2004: 89)

What kind of soundscape do Sirens, the Homeric and the technological inhabit? A space, sometimes privatized, between Odysseus and the Sirens, mimicked by contemporary smartphone users in Israel and elsewhere as users listen for warnings of missile attacks – both are intimate, Odysseus listening in the constructed privatized space between himself and the Sirens, while his oarsmen row on oblivious; one sound seduces, the other warns. But Odysseus has already been forewarned of the dangers of his sonic seduction – there is no risk entailed in listening.[1] For those who read the *Odyssey* or its subsequent hybrids and adaptations – it is an imaginary sonic space conjured up from the page. There exist no sonic vibrations in the reading of literature – merely imaginary vibrations. No one heard mythical Sirens sing out at sea before the age of mechanical reproduction – before experienced in early plays or operas as entertainments for the wealthy.[2] Sirens – voiceless – had resided on the walls of art galleries – as images only, or were represented in the silent films of Annette Kellermann, close enough to touch?[3] Today, 'Sirens' are audiovisualized on screen, seen on stage as they sing, or viewed dancing in 'strip-clubs' – all body, silent and 'up-close', or indeed read as coming-of-age novels for young women.⁴ These are the soundscapes of 'mythical' Sirens, largely liberated from the written page into everyday life and culture. Other kinds of siren are unencumbered by the West's literary Siren origins even though they take their name from it. These sirens move through city streets transforming the urban soundscape, a 'keynote' – sometimes overwhelming the soundscape, swamping it. Or represent a moment of calm, after the Hiroshima air-raid sirens signalled the *all-clear* on the morning of 6 August 1945; citizens looking skywards at the clear empty sky before the conflagration occurs – silent at its centre – beyond this the loudest sound known to 'man', the explosion blackening sky and land. Hiroshima transformed from a 'hi-fi' to a 'lo-fi' soundscape just like that.⁵

Sirens: From the Local to the Global

Three thousand years ago Homeric Sirens were located primarily in the minds of Greeks, some seafaring, some not. And while we might dispute the 'home' of Homeric Sirens as the Li Galli islands lying off the Bay of Sorrento, Sirens were nonetheless 'localized'. In the Greek imaginary most of the ocean was 'Siren free'. Homer's Sirens were not located at sea but were earth bound – singing from their 'meadow,' before them their male victims, tempted by their song, slowly rotting in their reveries. It is only the Sirens voices that reach beyond their island home and into the ears and minds of Odysseus or any other unaware sailors. The Sirens remained phantoms for those who listened – invisible – acousmatic. By the time Apollonius of Rhodes puts pen to paper some 300 years after Homer, the Sirens had become airborne and possessed names and a heritage.

> A moderate wind carried the ship forward, and soon they saw the lovely island of Anthemoessa where the clear-voiced Sirens, daughters of Acheloos, destroyed all who moored beside them with the enchantment of their sweet songs. Beautiful Terpsichore, one of the Muses, bore them after sharing Acheloos' bed, and once they had looked after the mighty daughter of Deo, while she was still a virgin, their voices mingled in song. When the Argonauts came, however, they looked in part like birds, and in

part like young girls. They kept a constant look-out from their perch in the lovely harbour: many indeed were the men whom they had deprived of their sweet return, destroying them with wasting desire. For the Argonauts too they opened their mouths in pure liquid song as soon as they saw them. (Appolinus 1993: 119–20)

Appolinus' Sirens have no need to touch their hapless victims; their song and their bodies 'destroy them with wasting desire'. The Argonauts are saved, not by wax, but by the playing of the lyre by Pan, who scrambles the sounds of the Sirens, reducing their potency. This scene, replicated on ancient Greek vases of the time, yet substituting Appolinus' Argonauts for the Homeric image of Odysseus tied to the mast of his ship, captivated by the three Siren-birds flying around his adoring, aching face. The image making, as early as the fifth century BCE, the imagination redundant; the visual replacing the acousmatic (Figure 7.1).

FIGURE 7.1 *Image from the British Museum Open Source Collection.*

The Sirens of myth gradually migrated from their meadow to the world beyond, travellers of sky, sea and land as they metamorphosed into half-bird half-woman, and then half-fish half-woman, luring hapless men to their deaths. Mythical Greek Sirens in moving beyond their original 'home' transformed Western culture's relationship to sound, place and gender. Yet even as the Siren myth travelled, it was itself the product of travel from Egypt and Assyria to Greece to become increasingly global through conquest, colonialism and, most recently, global popular culture.[6] With the creation of mermaids in popular literature they roamed the world's oceans in search of men and love pursuing them across the globe. Mermaids cropped up everywhere in the Western imagination. H. G. Wells wrote *The Sea Lady* at the beginning of the twentieth century portraying the mermaid as demure and sophisticated, possessing all of the behaviour and charms of a young English upper-class 'society' lady albiet with a non-detachable fishtail. She has come in search of Chatteris, a young would-be politician whom she had originally seen off the coast of Tonga. The novel is subsequently translated into the 1948 film *Miranda* starring Glynis Johns. In the Wells novel, narrated by Melville who is a cousin of Chatteris (his name an allusion to Moby Dick),[7] the mermaid comes ashore in Folkstone where the Chatteris family are spending their summer holiday. She manoeuvres to get herself rescued by the men in the family in order to ingratiate herself into Chatteris's family, and is originally accepted by the women in the family who are immediately taken by her, despite her fishtail – largely because of her sophistication and charm. Later in the novel *The Sea Lady* informs Melville about her first sighting of Chatteris:

'I saw him first', she apologised, 'some years ago'.

'Where?'

'In the South Seas – near Tonga'.

'And that is really what you came for?'

This time her manner was convincing. She admitted, 'Yes'. (Wells 2013: xxvi)

The mermaid and Chatteris disappear at the end of the novel, never to be seen again. Before this happens, Melville warns the Chatteris family: 'She comes out of the sea. ... Out of some other world. She comes, whispering that this life is a phantom life, unreal, flimsy, limited, casting upon everything a spell of disillusionment. ... She is a mermaid, she is a thing of dreams and desires, a siren, a whisper and a seduction. She will lure him with her' (Wells 2013: cxxi). Wells's mermaid parodies the respectable bourgeois woman or wife of the time, acting as its critique – Chatteris leaves behind his prospective wife, together with his bourgeois respectability and ambition, for the ocean and the mermaid. Its critique of the stifling opportunities and values available to middle-class women of the time makes it one of the more interesting mermaid novels of the time. But the primary point here is to note that Wells's mermaid is a creature of the world's oceans – the ocean home more exotic and freer than life that existed on land.

Interpreting Siren Spaces

Spaces of the past are frequently viewed through contemporary eyes. Homer's meadow from which the Sirens sing has been interpreted both literally and metaphorically in contemporary explanations of the Siren myth. Albrecht Wellmer in his discussion of Adorno's interpretation of the myth has suggested that the 'meadow' in Greek is a colloquial term for female genitals and that Circe's description of the Sirens as possessing 'voices like sweet honey' plays on the sexual nature of the encounter. The psychoanalytically inspired explanations of this placing of desire accepts the gendered nature of the tale in the manner of the nineteenth-century medical theorists who pursued the misogynist Siren agenda in their description of women as 'hysterics' governed by 'uncontrollable' sexual desires (Dijkstra 1998b).[8] Rebecca Comay extends the meadow metaphor of 'honeyed experience' more broadly to include many of the women or goddesses that Odysseus encounters in the *Odyssey*, 'the "honey sweet fruit" of the lotus flowers had made men forget the voyage home. Circe's beautiful song and honeyed wine made them forgetful of their fatherland. Calypso with her beguiling voice and nectar had promised immortality, but at the cost of fame. The Sirens' "honeyed voices", in contrast, promised a kind of memory, but at the cost of life' (Comay 2000: 25). Yet the association of 'honey' with the sexual body of a woman is not universally accepted, with Van Liefferinge claiming that a voice 'as sweet as honey' 'etymologically refers to divine inspiration' and refers to a poetic connection between the sirens and bees associated with a 'strong poetic and prophetic symbolism' during this period of Greek culture (Liefferinge 2012: 1). Liefferinge points to the status of the 'meadow' as a space, while not associated symbolically or materially with the bodies of Sirens, nevertheless is a place of death occurring elsewhere in Greek mythology as a place associated with the underworld described in Plato's *Republic* and elsewhere. Sloterdijk points to this extension of the role of Sirens beyond the *Odyssey* in Greek myth, 'the Sirens normally performed a lament for the dead. Their power is borrowed from the underworld and its lords, Hady's and Phorcys; hence their voices are especially suitable for hymns of praise and songs for the dead. Their foreknowledge concerns human destinies and their unknown end' (Sloterdijk 2011: 495). Plato also sketches out an alternative vision and purpose for the Sirens and the spaces they inhabit which has been largely neglected outside of Medieval Music and classical studies but which links more clearly with the present connection between mythical Siren places and those of twentieth-century sirens of war. As previously mentioned, Plato in the final section of the *Republic* discusses the myth of Er, in which he identifies a

> demonic location identified as a meadow at the intersection of four roads, or more precisely, twice two roads facing each other – two ascending to heaven and back downwards respectively, and two others descending to Hell and leading back upwards. This is where we find the judges who send souls on the way to heaven or on the road to the underworld. (Van Liefferinge 2012: 2)

For Plato, the meadow lies at the crossroads between heaven and hell and is where the souls of the dead lie before travelling up and down the paths leading to heaven and hell. On their journeying, these souls come to the Platonic Sirens who are suspended around the spindle of necessity which rotates the universe, 'eight orbits each of which create a perfect circle. ... Atop each circle, a Siren sings a single note, and the ensemble is in harmony. ... The Sirens are eight in number, corresponding to the cosmos and the seven planets, and their song, each note on the octave, is a harmonious whole-the famous music of the spheres' (Van Liefferinge 2012: 5).

Plato's 'angelic', non-sexual Sirens subsequently feature in medieval thought whereby the nature of music on the earth and Cosmos and everything in it is formed as a rational whole. More directly, Sirens in Euripides are represented as companions of the souls of the dead leading them to the underworld. This view of their mediating role between life and death is apparent in the portrayal of Sirens adorning many Greek tombs. Plutarch claimed that the role of the Sirens was to sooth through music,

> the power of music is neither fatal nor inhuman, but that in the souls that have left here to go below and wander after death, it brings forth love for heavenly and divine things and the forgetting of mortal things, it charms and possesses them in song, and they under the influence of that joy, accompany and follow their revolutions [as in Plato's Sirens on the spindle of necessity]. And here, as a faint echo of the music reaches us and calls our souls with poetry, it reminds them of the realities that precede from it. (Van Liefferinge 2012: 9)

These alternative Greek visions of the role that Sirens played in life and death and the status of their 'meadow' home have not captured the imagination of subsequent generations. While the Sirens of Greek mythology gradually migrated from their earthly home of the meadow and metamorphosed into creatures of the skies and seas, their role in the Homeric sense of luring sailors to their death through the enticements of their song remained. By the nineteenth century, their sounds were transformed with the invention of the mechanical siren – a warning to sailors at sea of danger, their purpose to guide them to safety. A benevolent sound, but just as the acousmatic sounds of Homer's Sirens failed to lure Odysseus and his crew to their demise, early sirens often failed to effectively warn sailors of dangers at sea.[9] Yet, these sounds become less benevolent as they metamorphize into air-raid sirens. As I have argued in this book, the sounds of sirens cannot be understood in isolation from the world that creates them, just as mythical Sirens cannot be divorced from the misogyny within which they were created, reinvented and perpetuated.

However the spaces of mythical Sirens are interpreted – the meadow on which they sit and sing are meadows of death – leading either to an abyss, the underworld, or indeed the heavens. Their more recent and secular versions have flown and swam and exist over all of Earth – which paradoxically is transformed into their 'meadow'. In the twentieth century when a sanitized Siren culture is more often a product of Disney films or teenage fiction, it is not the Sirens of myth that enticed unwary men to their deaths on the meadows of Earth but the weapons of mass destruction signalled by the howling of air-raid sirens, not the enticements of Homer's Sirens or the calming symmetry of those of Plato, informing the earth's inhabitants to flee for their lives. This tale of horror has been told many times by those who survived from the mass killings of the twentieth century in which any space could become a killing field. As previously discussed, Kurt Vonnegut recounts this experience in his novel *Slaughterhouse 5*, 'The air raid sirens of Dresden howled mournfully. The Americans and their guards and Campbell took shelter in an echoing meat locker which was hollowed in living rock under the slaughterhouse. There was an iron staircase with iron doors at the top and bottom' (Vonnegut 2019: 135). Vonnegut and the other prisoners were in their own underworld. After the night of aerial killing Vonnegut emerges from this underworld and is told to bury the remains of the dead and because there are too many to incinerate them, 'I dug corpses from cellars and carried them, unidentified, their names recorded nowhere, to monumental funeral pyres. Their corpses could have been anybody, including me, and there were surely representative among them, whether collaborators or slaves or refugees, of every nation involved in the European half of World War 2' (Vonnegut in P. Beidler Vol XLIX, Issue 1 2010: p8).

While in the nineteenth century warning sirens were initially orientated towards the sea, they migrated to land in the twentieth century, in reverse direction to those of myth. While Vonnegut heard the sounds of the air-raid sirens from his abattoir, the inhabitants of Hiroshima had no underground shelters. And while it took 800 bombers all night to destroy Dresden, just a few months later those who lived in Hiroshima would be visited by a weapon that no siren or bunker could prove effective against. On the morning of 6 August 1945, John Hersey recounts the story of Mr Tanimoto, a resident of Hiroshima, who was the chairman of his local civil defence team whose responsibility it was to organize the local air-raid defences. Mr Tanimoto could read the meaning of the various air-raid sirens that formed a part of the city's defence system. On that morning he had luckily left home early, accompanied by a friend, on an errand to the outskirts of the city:

> A few minutes after they started, the air-raid siren went off – a minute long blast that warned of approaching planes but indicated to the people of Hiroshima only a slight degree of danger, since it sounded every morning at this time, when an American weather plane came over. ... As they started up a valley away from the tight-ranked houses, the all-clear sounded. ... There was no sound of planes. The morning was still; the place cool and pleasant. Then a tremendous flash of light cut across the sky. He heard no roar [almost no one in Hiroshima recall hearing any noise of the bomb]. (Hersey 1946 [2001]: 7–9)

At 8.16 am the atomic bomb exploded above Hiroshima. Within a minute an estimated 70,000 people were dead – incinerated – blown off the face of the earth with an equal number subsequently dying in the aftermath – the quickest and largest man-made death toll in human history. The sirens that Mr Tanimoto heard warned citizens of attack in order that they may take protective measures. They were a subordinate clause in the values and aims of 'total war' in which any space might become a 'meadow' of death.

Everybody with hearing can hear sirens, even those who are deaf might feel their vibration. These warning sirens are more democratic than the mythical sirens that are merely heard by men. This apparent modern democracy of sound might be understood as part of a 'negative dialectic' whereby all fall under the sonic spell of the siren – men, women and children – it is not the siren that destroys them – the siren is not representing itself – but the weapons and values that it purports to protect citizens from. It is the logic of domination articulated in the *Dialectic of Enlightenment* and extends from the domination of nature, gender and culture into universal destructiveness. As Adorno noted, from the slingshot to the atom bomb in which the siren blares out *'as if'* it could make a difference. The dialectical entwining of myth, power and destructiveness in which the wound is cognitive, bodily and spatial – extending from Homer to Hiroshima *'and beyond'*.

8

Hearing the Sirens

A Tale of Sonic Exclusivity?

Our ability to place siren sounds have always been subject to the vagaries of atmospheric conditions, geographical and physical topology, our own placing and our own sense of hearing and experience. Prior to sirens, bells had sometimes fulfilled the same function to sonically warn. Murray Schafer, for many, the founder of sound studies, made the connection between the bell and the siren in terms of a perceived sonic evolutionism governed by technology. Schafer noted that both technologies – the bell and the siren, 'radiates energy in all directions uniformly', with aims that differ yet overlap. He believed that, 'sirens and church bells belong to the same class of sounds: they are community signals. As such they must be loud enough to emerge clearly out of the ambient noise of the community. But while the church bell sets a protective spell on the community, the siren speaks of disharmony from within' (Schafer 1994: 178). This disharmony of industrial sound, embodied, for Schafer, in the technology of the siren situates such a sonic technology within his understanding of its power to transform the soundscape and subordinate the subject within a dominating sonic matrix of 'industry, transportation and war, power over nature and power over other men' (Schafer 1994: 179). Schafer, while lacking the dialectical acumen of Theodor Adorno and Max Horkheimer in their critique of the Enlightenment, nevertheless focuses upon the power of the sonic in the transformation of cultural practices, assumptions and formations. Schafer understands the siren as denoting an internal disharmony representative of industrial culture – in this he appears to be referring to the sirens used by police forces that pierce the urban air with warning.

In contrast to Schafer's industrial sirens, air-raid sirens, like the church bell, attempted, albeit ideologically, to place a 'protective spell' over its community; any disharmony came not from within but from without. The idea of sonic inclusivity and warning, articulated by the role of air-raid sirens for many inhabitants of cities in the twentieth century is also central to Alain Corbin's study of the nineteenth-century French village bell. For Corbin this sonic inclusivity was defined geographically. The sounds of a pealing bell drawing in a lost ship in the fog of night or a lost traveller from the mists of the forest create an enduring image of the inclusivity that sound potentially has, of sound 'drawing in' the subject to the safety of a community. In Finistere, for example, the church bell rang out 'to signal to sailors the precise location of the coastline in times of thick fog, which obscured the lighthouse' (Corbin 1998: 101). Corbin's bells, unlike Schafer's sirens, are largely rural – pre-urban, although they continue in various parts of the world to call the faithful to prayer. For Corbin, the village bell was placed at the cultural and moral centre of the villager's aural landscape. They were highly specific pieces of technology, modulated so that they could be heard anywhere in the village commune.[1] The sound of the bell – each with its own distinctive and recognizable timbre – was the gate, fencing in the local population and contributing to their sense of place and identity – inclusive, yet separate from those beyond the peal of the bell. Their localized 'difference' of timbre representing cultural uniformity. As such, the bell symbolized roots and identity in a world dominated by the slow rhythms of the seasons and the fixity of place. Corbin also charted the partial disintegration of the communal bell as French society urbanized and became increasingly secular. The bell no longer necessarily representing the 'romantic' unified identity described by Schafer, but a more polarized divisive aural sphere as sections of the population found the pealing of the bell intrusive and culturally irrelevant. The relatively fixed spaces of habitation of the village commune gave way to the mobile and transitory spaces of modernity articulated in the sociology of Ferdinand Tonnies, Emile Durkheim and Georg Simmel.

The bell and the air-raid siren both periodically co-existed and served similar social and sonic objectives. Both ironically were fixed, the one in the church tower, the other atop city buildings – both aimed to reach everybody in the locale albeit primarily in cities and not village communities; both aimed at, or signified, the creation of 'a protective shell' over the subject community. Yet, the movement of sonic warnings and their technological development from the church bell to the air-raid siren from village to city is a phenomenon of the twentieth century, representing a moral and technological inflected development of a dialectic of power and protectiveness.

Schafer's sonic inclusivity of the past itself remains ideological and partial. While Murray Schafer hears a poverty of contemporary sounds, he simultaneously waxes lyrical about the allure of the American Frontier with the sound of the train: 'By comparison with the sound of modern transportation, those of the trains were rich and characteristic: the whistle, the bell, the slow chuffing of the engine at the start. ... The sounds of travel have deep mysteries. ... The trains whistle was the most important sound in the frontier town, the solo announcement of contact with the outside world' (Schafer 1979 [1994]: 81). Schafer appears 'blind' to the use of the railway in its role within the imperialist expansion of Native American land. Early American settlers, as indeed Schafer, are silent on the role of train expansion in the resettlement of Native American tribes in order to facilitate the laying of railway tracks between 1840 and 1880, or the railroads' role in the opening up of the Great Plains for commercial hide trading which saw the extinction of bison, an important part of Native American livelihood, over the subsequent years. There are virtually no American Indian accounts of the coming of, or the sound of the railways.

Equally, air-raid sirens in their heyday in the Second World War did not sound for everyone. Just as the air-raid sirens of Dresden did not sound for Kurt Vonnegut, they did not sound for the fifteen-year-old Helga Weiss as she was being transported by train from Terezin to Auschwitz in 1944. Her sirens existed on the edge of consciousness, attempting to locate their sounds from her moving blacked out cattle carriage, packed, standing room only, with others moving towards their end, a different 'killing' field from those announced by the air-raid sirens. From the darkness, Helga hears a distant air-raid siren and knows she's in Germany: 'The train stopped for a while. No, now its flying onward – that was a siren, there must be an air raid somewhere. What if it hits here? We're in Germany now, there are air raids here' (Weiss 2014: 67).

No sirens were sounded for the European Jews of Paris, Berlin, Hamburg and other European cities during the Second World War. The sirens, while sounded for the home populations, were not for them; there was to be no protection, sonic or otherwise, from the countries within which they lived. For the Jews, death would come to the strains of 'Rosamunde', a popular song played to the inmates of Auschwitz and Majdanek as they were killed (Gilbert 2005). The myth of unified subject collectivities based on physical spaces articulated in the work of Schafer, Corbin and others was laid bare, at the very time in which states were proclaiming it.

Paradoxically, Israel today is awash with air-raid sirens that perform a dual role: one is traditional, warning its inhabitants of incoming missiles; the other is a mode of 'collective commemoration' within the Israeli state. Sirens are sounded throughout Israel on three days each year: Holocaust Memorial Day, the Memorial Day for Fallen Soldiers, and Independence Day, when many Israelis pay their respects in silence as the sirens wail.

Contemporary Israel appears to hark back to the sonic unity embodied in Alain Corbin's bells of the nineteenth century, out of yet in time, with the same ideology of collective unity that fails to name the excluded within its borders. During these three days, the Israeli media focus almost exclusively on the national cultural significance of the day. As Danny Kaplan writes,

> In this sense, the radio broadcast disseminates and magnifies the quality of 'selfless unisonance', as experienced, for instance, by the audience singing the anthem during national ceremonies, and in the Israeli case is especially apparent in the piercing, awe-inspiring unisonance of the sirens. The majority who choose not to participate in the ceremonies and carry on with their daily lives nevertheless encounter the uniform memorial music wherever they go and are thus exposed to the same commemorative mode and mood nonetheless. (Kaplan 2009: 321)

And sirens are sounded in the traditional mode to warn of imminent attack via rudimentary missiles fired from Palestine – hence, returning to a pre-nuclear period in which the air-raid siren could still have some legitimacy as a sonic warning system. Israelis have between fifteen and ninety seconds of warning to move into their air-raid shelters, depending on where they live in relation to the Palestinian border. The government system of public sonic warning is supplemented by the development of a range of mobile apps – a privatization of the air-raid siren that exists in parallel to the official public system. One such app, Red Alert, became Israel's most popular download during the bombing campaign of 2012, with some users such as Israela Natan, claiming, 'It just gives [you] that extra bit of information that makes [you] feel like [you're] still in control' (Hod 2014: 5). This is similar to the response of traditional iPod users when they discuss the power of privatized music to influence their feelings of well-being (Bull 2007). These mobile apps produced conflicting responses among users that ranged from feelings of anxiety and inattention to feelings of security – the constant yet private response to sonic warnings in the twenty-first century.

9

Sirens for the Young

From Fénelon to Disney

The story is a simple one, the main character, a young girl aged twelve – her name is Lorelie – a name with some historical pedigree in the history of mermaids. She has three older sisters, Lara, Lula and Lily who work in the local family diner – they are Sirens – and appear as normal teenage girls apart from the fish scales on the bottom of their feet. Lorelie doesn't want to become a Siren – which she will at the age of thirteen. She is in love with a young boy called Jason whose stepfather owns the local harbour and boats on which he will sail – it is a seafaring town and she lives in fear that on turning thirteen she will lure him to his death on the rocks. The novel begins as Lorelie reluctantly watches her sisters lure a ship onto the coastline rocks with their singing, 'My sisters hold hands and begin to sing. Their voices are pure and perfect, and their song is so sweet you can practically taste it' (Langer 2017: 2). The novel proceeds as a quest in which Lorelie tries to avert her fate and become human. It has the usual character of the 'Sea Witch', recognizable from the Walt Disney mermaid movies, who controls her sisters and, increasingly, Lorelie. In her quest, Lorelie discovers a 300-year-old diary written by a Siren, Hannah, who was sentenced to death for being a witch. The 300-year time span is derived from the Hans Christian Andersen story 'The Little Princess' written in the early years of the nineteenth century – the length of time a mermaid lives, unless she obtains a human soul through the love of a man. Lorelie reads from the diary, 'When Rebecca comes home safely, then, perhaps, I will recite this spell for forgiveness and reunite the broken pieces of my soul. Then, perhaps, I will find peace. And then I shall set them [the sirens] all free' (Langer 2017: 230). It transpires that the Sea Witch transforms young girls into Sirens in exchange for giving life to another, she discovers that her three sisters did this for her after she had died in a car crash, 'All this time, I thought my sisters wanted to be beautiful and powerful and immortal. But that's not what happened at all. They did it for me. When I died, they were right there in the graveyard with a flashlight, and a shovel, and a spell from the Sea Witch. They were willing to trade their own lives just to bring me back' (230). They discover the spell to make Hannah whole again, making an apology by the sea for the townsfolk who had killed Hannah so long ago thereby enabling the sisters themselves to return to human form. Langer's story is both a coming-of-age novel and a morality play in which the young girls became Sirens for moral reasons – and it is through their moral principles that they return to human form. The tale is also normatively heterosexual as all other Siren and mermaid tales and draws selectively from the Siren tradition, less so Homer, more from De La Motte Fouqué's *Undine* and Hans Christian Andersen filtered through the lens of Walt Disney. Contemporary literature is 'awash' with Sirens. Contemporary Siren literature is the domain of young female authors who write for the young female market. They occupy the space of traditionally male authors – yet paradoxically do little to transform the myth itself. A recent example is *The Siren* – what else – written by Kiera Cass (2016) in which the leading character – a young woman, Kahlen, sells her soul to the ocean for 100 years in order to save her own life. In exchange for her life, she leads others to their deaths through her song. The book retains the tradition of the myth by invoking Kahlen's voice as an instrument of death. However, she falls in love with a young handsome boy – Akinli – but she cannot speak with him, thus retaining the silencing of the mermaid from Hans Christian Andersen. The novel predictably descends into a tale of young love adorned with shopping trips and wealthy living arrangements as a backdrop to the tale in what appears akin to wealthy students embarking on the adventures of their Gap Year with eventually Kahlen saving Akinli's life from the clutches of the Sea Witch, thereby maintaining an ambiguous moral pose, devoid of economic base; we never discover how the Sirens pay for their luxuries, coupled with an exclusive heterosexual normative expectation.

These Siren instruction manuals for young girls, for this is what they are, goes back to the seventeenth century, before the stories of Hans Christian Andersen and others. These accounts tended to focus upon the adventurous sequences of the Odyssey which included the Siren episode and it was these that held the imaginative appeal of the young. Francesca Richards argues that 'children's versions of the Odyssey have fundamentally contributed to this privileging of the adventure episodes of the Homeric epic in a wider context: an understanding that continues to persist in the popular imagination' (Richards 2016: 7). Of central importance to this historical narrative for the young is Fénelon's *The Adventures of Telemachus* translated into English in 1699 which was quickly introduced into the UK school curriculum of the time and was widely read representing the singular moment of introducing the Sirens into Western popular consciousness.

Fénelon rewrote the *Odyssey* from the perspective of Telemachus, Odysseus's son, who goes in search of his father. It is no accident that the book is titled *The Adventures of Telemachus*, Fénelon like many subsequent authors and film-makers concentrated on the 'fantastic' nature of the Odyssey stressing the nature of the 'encounter, struggle and survival' of Telemachus as something that would find favour with the reader, especially younger male readers. Fénelon, unlike most subsequent popularizers of the *Odyssey* included political and philosophical issues into the text – directing the reader to wider and topical concerns (Richards 2016). Fénelon, as in other rewritings, includes a Siren episode in his text. While adventure ranks highly in the entertainment factor of Fénelon's account there remains a focus upon song as a form of temptation to men and disparaging descriptions of women and goddesses who engage in singing throughout the text. Telemachus is portrayed as an inexperienced and naïve adolescent who is guided through his adventures by his friend Mentor into becoming a mature, honest and courageous man by the end of the tale, rather than the sexually rapacious Odysseus. Telemachus is a male 'coming-of-age' novel differing from Hans Christian Andersen's tale and subsequent iterations as a female 'coming-of-age' story. Telemachus is shipwrecked on the island where Calypso reigns and on which she had had an affair with Odysseus. On meeting Telemachus, she is immediately attracted to him. Mentor councils Telemachus against her saying that he should not 'delight in gaudy ornaments like a weak woman' to which

Telemachus replies, 'the son of Ulysses shall never be vanquished by the charms of a base effeminate life' (Fénelon 6). After supper, Calypso wines and dines Telemachus with Fénelon setting the scene of the evening in sonic terms with the singing of 'nymphs' who sexually charge the atmosphere mixing love with knowledge: 'At the same time four young nymphs began to tune their voices. First they sang of the battle of the gods against the giants; then the amours of Jupiter and Semele; the birth of Bacchus. ... At length the war of Troy was likewise sung, and the valor and wisdom of Ulysses extolled to the skies' (Fénelon 1699: 6–7). It is clear from Fénelon that a major task of a young man growing to be a person of virtue is to avoid the deceitful sexual advances of 'base' women. These early tales were not orientated to young women however but to young men who were meant to read Fénelon's account as a saga of how a boy should grow into a responsible and 'moral' young man. The socialization of young women had to wait until the rewriting of the myth by Friedrich de la Motte Fouqué and Hans Christian Andersen over one hundred years later.

The endowing of moral precepts read into the *Odyssey* predates Fénelon's account with the various episodes of the *Odyssey* frequently referring to different virtues and temptations. This separation encouraged a reading of the *Odyssey* in terms of its separate parts – as a set of adventures. Richards demonstrates that from Erasmus onwards the *Odyssey* was disassembled 'but the fragments themselves, removed from their original context, were freed to take on a life of their own, in both Erasmus and the works of others' (Richards 2016: 28). Postmodernism appears alive and well in the fifteenth century.

Charles Lamb, writing in the shadow of Fénelon, published *The Adventures of Ulysses* in 1808 turning the Odyssey into an exciting series of adventures to be read by the young. The Siren episode is similar to that of Homer, although the language is more direct, with Circe warning Odysseus, 'There the deathful Sirens lie in wait for, that taint the minds of whoever listens to them with their sweet singing ... the celestial harmony of the voices which sang them [the verses] no tongue can describe: it took the ear of Ulysses with ravishment' (Lamb 1808: 11). Lamb twists Homer's account by having Circe in league with the Sirens, thus doubly exposing Odysseus to the 'deceit' of women, 'As well she might speak of them, for often she had joined her own enchanting voice to theirs, while she sat in the flowery meads, mingled with the Sirens and the Water Nymphs, gathering their potent herbs and drugs of magic quality: their singing altogether has made the gods stoop, and "heaven drowsy with harmony"' (Lamb 1808: 11).

The theme of the deception of the Sirens and temptation they hold for men, and the later sacrifice of the mermaid for the love of her man are the two socializing tropes embedded in Siren novels and films. The mermaids of Andersen and Disney are defined by their lack – lack of a soul and subsequently lack of their voice. They are however 'moral' creatures who die to save their unfaithful love, 'His wedding morning would bring death to her, and she would change into the foam of the sea' (Andersen: 10). Andersen partially redeems the mermaid as a reward for her virtue, while in Disney they of course survive and are united with their loved one – in life to live happily ever after.

Since the inception of film, Sirens and Mermaids have commonly been represented – yet if the role of film is to adapt myth into other times and places then these adaptations have in the main been uninspiring, representing the Siren myth literally or translating it via Hans Christian Andersen's 'The Little Mermaid' and other nineteenth-century fictional narratives.

A trace of Fénelon's *The Tales of Telemachus* extends beyond the teen movie feeding into adult-orientated filmic representation of Sirens. In Fénelon's tale, Pygmalion is seeking to capture Telemachus due to his alien status in his kingdom – Narbel, the captain of Pygmalion's ship, seeks to help Telemachus by telling him to lie about his origins in order that he might escape. Telemachus refuses to do so citing the woman Astarbe as an example not to follow,

> That woman was beautiful as a goddess; to the charms of her person she joined some engaging qualities of the mind, being sprightly, and insinuating. Notwithstanding these deceitful charms, she, like the Sirens, had a cruel and malignant heart; but she knew how to disguise her corrupt sentiments. By her beauty, her wit, her fine voice, and with her skill in touching the lyre, she had captivated the heart of Pygmalion who, in consequence of his blind passion for her, had forsaken his queen Topha. (Fénelon 1699: 41)

It is but a short distance to the more 'universal' category of Siren as 'femme-fatale' articulated in much of film noir – a more adult, but equally repressive, education.

10

Kafka's Sirens and the Story of Silencing

A young woman must charm. She must become a siren.
(ABBA WOOLSON 1870)

The air-raid sirens of Dresden and Hiroshima were silenced by the deadly technologies of the state, they had begun life as sonic warnings for all to hear. The Siren song of myth, however, began in silence, on the written page as literature. Their representation on ancient vases, reliefs and paintings from antiquity to the present day are viewed not 'heard'– the sonic merely residing in the viewer's imagination, if at all. Kata Gellen claims, in response to the 'silence' of the written word when it refers to sounds, that 'literary theory … has no means of theorising sound, nor sound studies, which has shown little interest in literary narrative' (Gellen 2019: 7). This statement appears disingenuous. Literary theory has engaged extensively with the representation of a wide range of sonically based experience, especially urban experience and more recently with innovative studies on the sounding of race in literature (Keskinen 2008; Mathes 2015; Schweighauser 2006; Smith 1999; St Clair 2013, 2018; Stoever 2016). Literature is reflective of the wider social processes which include its contextualization and understanding of the role the sonic plays in representing power and modernity. Sound manifests itself cognitively in the act of reading as it might in the act of gazing at the paintings of Sirens in the art galleries of the world. Sound is embodied in literature and the representative arts, just as it is in music, theatre and film. The relationship of the arts to 'everyday' life is also intimately connected; the shift from the telling of stories in literature to the manifestation of forms of Siren misogyny in daily life is but a short distance (Dijkstra 1986).

While the Siren episode in Homer's *Odyssey* primarily concerns itself with the representation of 'sonic' temptation manifested, depending on the critique, either as 'sound' itself, sound as knowledge or nature, manifested as flesh. In this trace the focus is upon strategies embodied in the silencing the Sirens – not in the sense of the separating of literature from the social, or in the claim that literature is itself 'silent' (Blanchot 2003) – but rather literally, metaphorically and culturally.

The analysis of the 'silencing' of the Sirens begins with the work of Franz Kafka rather than with the more popular Hans Christian Andersen's, 'The Little Mermaid' or indeed Walt Disney with his mermaid adaptations of Andersen and others. Kafka's short story 'Silence of the Sirens' has received more critical analysis than any other 'modern' story that concerns itself with the Sirens of myth. Kafka's centrality within the pantheon of modernist writing might well account for this, as against the more *popular* cultural terrain of Andersen or Disney. Even within the realm of modernist discourse we frequently find ourselves confronting the 'Silence of the Sirens' rather than, for example, Kurt Vonnegut's *The Sirens of Titan* – arguably a more profound and lengthy meditation on the role and meaning of Sirens in an 'imaginary' social setting – but Vonnegut's work of course is mere 'science fiction'. The present work suspends these literary and cultural distinctions to focus the analysis on the social and cultural meanings of the sonic within these Siren portrayals in order to interrogate the nature and meanings of their 'silencing' of the Sirens.

Kafka wrote 'Silence of the Sirens' in 1917 – one of many literary reinterpretations of Homer's Siren episode written at that time. Kafka uniquely keeps to the same length as Homer in his telling of the tale. Despite its brevity the story remains culturally important despite Kafka's broader and arguably more significant engagement with the sonic in other work such as the 'The Burrow', a wonderful account of acousmatic sound; and in 'Josephine the Singer' in which he questions the nature of the voice and its reception, and indeed in his letters where he comments broadly on his encounters with the sonic. Yet it is with 'Silence of the Sirens' that Kafka becomes, in contrast to his other work, very much a 'man' of his time.

Kafka's 'Silence of the Sirens' offers a dramatic transformation of Homer's original account of Odysseus's encounter with the Sirens and it is precisely his sonic transformation of the tale which is of interest here. In Kafka's retelling, Odysseus fills his ears with wax along with his crew, unlike in the original, where Odysseus ears remain open. Despite Odysseus having closed his ears, he remains tied to the mast of his ship as in the Homeric tale. The resulting transformation of the episode results in Kafka reprioritizing the visual in Odysseus's encounter with the Sirens while simultaneously dismissing the sonic within the encounter. Kafka portrays the Sirens as deciding not to sing – as enigmatically – they think that their 'silence' is 'more powerful' than their song, and besides, Kafka observes somewhat literally, wax would have proven ineffective in protecting Odysseus and his crew from the Siren's song, if indeed they had decided to sing. The sonic would have proven a distraction, for Kafka, to the mutual entrancement that the Sirens and Odysseus had for one another – an entrancement based entirely on the visual, 'he thought they were singing and that he alone did not hear them. For a fleeting moment he saw their throats rising and falling, their breasts lifting, their eyes filled with tears, their lips half parted, but believed that these were accompaniments to the airs which died unheard around him'. Odysseus sails on,

> and at the very moment when they were nearest to him he knew of them no longer. But they – lovelier than ever – stretched their necks and turned, let their awesome hair flutter free in the wind, and freely stretched their claws on the rocks. They no longer had any desire to allure; all they wanted was to hold as long as they could the radiance that fell from Odysseus' great eyes. (Kafka 2005: 431)

While literary theorists continue to argue about the potential cultural and psychoanalytical meaning of Kafka's tale in which it is the Sirens who are attracted to the vision of Odysseus, the present analysis argues that this reversal, based around 'sight', should not be divorced from the act of 'silencing' the Sirens in the retelling of the tale.

An alternative route to explaining this silencing of the Sirens is to point to Kafka's interest in early silent cinema thereby re-engaging Kafka with popular forms of entertainment and media technologies. Gellen argues that we should interpret 'Silence of the Sirens' in terms of silent cinema's portrayal of film stars, and of women in particular, in which extreme physical and expressive gestures were used to convey meaning – just as in the Kafka quotations mentioned earlier. Gellen argues that these gestures convey meaning in the *absence* of sound. Gellen understands Kafka's literary presentation of the Sirens as a literary mirror image of the visual spectacle which cinema audiences of the time experienced as 'real'. An essential component of this experience, she argues, was a complicity in the 'sonic deceit' represented on screen. Silent cinema for Gellen becomes an early example of lip-synching: 'Kafka's sirens also seem to comment on the status of divas and the phenomenon of stardom. The treacherous beauty of their twisted limbs, tuning torsos, wild hair, and sharp claws conforms *entirely* to the image of the mid 1910s silent film diva – melancholy, dangerous, self-destructive, and above all a *sight* to be *seen*' (Gellen 2019: 56, italics added).

In pursuit of tracing the connection between Kafka and silent cinema spectatorship Gellen chooses to ignore the sonic, and by extension the 'acousmatic' nature of the encounter in Homer, thereby reducing the Sirens in accordance with Kafka, to mere bodily posture represented as the source of desire. While Gellen might be correct in her portrayal of silent films representation of the 'diva', the move from Siren to 'diva' to 'woman' remains problematic. While the joining of Siren, to singer, to woman has increasingly been made in a range of academic writing, they equally fail to adequately address or resolve issues surrounding accounts of the nature of the 'male gaze' and more recently the 'female gaze'. Gellen's description of 'sexually provocative' females watched in silence in cinemas was not merely a phenomenon restricted to the cinema but was replicated, at the time of Kafka's writings, in a wide range of cultural productions; the art galleries of the West were overflowing with images of Sirens, nymphs and other creatures that supposedly populated the oceans, the products of the male and sometimes the female psyche. Fully voiced, yet 'dangerous', women were common fare in the opera houses of the world from Wagner's *Ring* Cycle, Dvorak's *Rusalka*, Strauss's *Salome*, Puccini's *Turandot* to Berg's *Lulu* while in literature Sirens proliferated in the writings of Johann

Goethe, Clemens Brentano, Oscar Wilde, H. G. Wells, James Joyce, Rainer-Maria Rilke and many other writers who were queuing up to write about Sirens and mermaids. Gellen, in disconnecting Kafka's tale from wider non-filmic representations of Sirens of the time, appears to endorse the misogyny embedded in Kafka's story rather than critiquing it. Dijkstra, in evaluating the representation of Siren episodes in Victorian and fin-de-siècle culture, gives greater credence to both the visual and the sonic nature of female representation of the time whilst pointing to its overwhelmingly misogynistic character: 'The symphonic incantations of ever newly curved female bodies were like the choral movements of a satanic invitation to worldly abandon. Women offered melodies of cradled melancholy to the labouring brain of sainted masculinity. Steely – browed and lean loined Ulysses sailed past these aching calls, seeking financial self-sufficiency among the shoals of vice' (Dijkstra 1986: 235).

Dijkstra's description appears close to Kafka's concerns of the time, as his letters appear to demonstrate. Kafka's retelling of the myth is in full accordance with the standard cultural representation of women in the culture of the time – and as such, ironically, it is one of his least 'imaginative' pieces of writing. Rather than focusing upon Kafka's interest in silent cinema as the source of his representation of Sirens others have pointed to a similarity between Kafka's story and his own letters to his fiancé, Felice Bauer, written during the same period of time as the conception and writing of the piece. During this time Kafka carried out an intense four-year distant 'romantic' correspondence with Bauer. Kafka was living in Prague while Bauer lived in Berlin resulting in infrequent 'physical' meetings due partially to geography but primarily due to Kafka's reticence. Kafka's letters, numbering two or three a day have survived while his letters to Bauer appeared to have been destroyed, perhaps by Kafka who may have thought them inconsequential or by Max Brod who managed Kafka's estate after his death. Kafka and Bauer's relationship, such as it was, produced two engagements before Kafka finally broke it off and existed primarily through letters and in the imagination of both of them. These letters, often monologues concerning Kafka's insecurities, his writing, his bodily disgust, his looks and sensitivities coupled with a heckling insistence as to how Bauer should engage her time productively. Elias Canetti believed that for the most part, Bauer had no idea what the young and unknown Kafka was talking about in many of his letters (Canetti 2012 [1974]). Kafka would perhaps recognize the meaning of Leonard Cohen lyric, 'I'm so sorry for the ghost I made you be, Only one of us was real – and that was me' (Cohen 2016). The male creation of woman as imaginary 'other' appears to remain alive and well in the popular culture of today. Kafka's fear of emotional attachment at that time is well documented – preferring to engage with women through writing rather than physical presence, 'You once said you would like to sit beside me while I write. Listen, in that case I would not write. ... For writing means revealing oneself to excess. ... This is why one can never be alone enough when one writes, why there can never be enough silence around one when one writes' (Kafka 2005: 155). Just as in Kafka's representation of the Sirens' attraction to Odysseus, it appears that it is Kafka who is the muse and Bauer who looks adoringly on in Kafka's imagination. In accordance with many other middle-class males of the time and in parallel to Kafka's virtual 'construction' of Bauer, he also visited prostitutes which he describes in his diaries, 'I purposely walk through streets where the whores are. It excites me to pass by them, that distant but still real possibility of going with one of them' (Stach 2016). Reiner Stach, Kafka's biographer, notes that the practice of visiting prostitutes was not considered a 'moral' issue at the time, by men at least. Kafka, along with Max Brod, his friend and editor, visited bordellos regularly in their travels to Milan, Paris and Leipzig (Stach 2016: 61). Elizabeth Boa points to the paradox of Kafka, his Sirens story and his relationship with Bauer, 'For muse and Sirens alike really inhabit the male artist's head: the woman must be silent or dead lest she retard the man on his creative journey. Kafka's letters to Felice confirm [this], for they make quite explicit that Kafka can only write if the woman is absent' (Boa 2004: 15). In the absence of Bauer's letters to Kafka she remains silent, just as Kafka's Sirens remain silent, both admiring of Kafka, their muse. Elsewhere in Kafka's life they remain mere body as art imitates life.

The silencing of the Sirens can take brutal physical form. Beyond Homer it was thought that the 'failed' Sirens would cast themselves into the ocean and die as punishment for their failure. In the influential Hans Christian Andersen fairy tale, the precursor to the Disney mermaid movies of the twentieth century, the mermaid literally has her tongue cut off so that she can no longer speak or sing – in Andersen's story, the mermaid, in accordance with

Kafka, becomes pure 'body'. In addition, for Andersen the Sirens of Greek myth metamorphose into mermaids which possess, rather than the 'predatory' instincts of Sirens, a set of domestic identities and desires.[1] While Kafka's Sirens remain dangerous, silent yet ultimately defeated – the parallel path of mermaids in popular culture is primarily one of young love thwarted – there is little danger invoked from the well-meaning mermaid towards the object of her love – a young handsome prince – of course. While Andersen's tale ends unhappily for the mermaid as the prince marries another, its Disney remake produces a contrived happy ending. The Disney movies, in accordance with the artwork accompanying the many editions of Hans Christian Andersen's story, portray mermaids as possessing a fishtail but no claws, is archetypally 'beautiful' and invariably 'blonde'. While Andersen maintains the beautiful song narrative of Sirens, they present none of the subversive undertones of Homer's Sirens. Indeed the mermaids merely sing about the beauty of ocean life to sailors who are in peril, while the listening sailors interpret their song, not as beautiful, but as the 'howling of the storm'. Andersen's mermaid saves her prince from drowning, falls in love with him and wishes to marry him. Her tail remains an impediment so she visits an 'ugly' witch (of course) who can transform her unsuitable tail into a fine pair of legs. The price of the exchange is both expensive and painful for the mermaid.

> 'But I must be paid also', said the witch, 'and it is not a trifle that I ask. You have the sweetest voice of any who dwell here in the depths of the sea, and you believe that you will be able to charm the prince with it also, but this voice you must give to me, the best thing you possess will I have.'
>
> 'But if you take away my voice', said the little mermaid, 'what is left for me?'
>
> 'Your beautiful form, your graceful walk, and your expressive eyes; surely with these you can enchain a man's heart. Well, have you lost your courage? Put out your little tongue that I may cut it off as my payment.' (Hans Christian Andersen: 8)

In addition to the loss of her voice the mermaid suffers from the pain of using her newly created legs – as if she were treading on knives. The ending is ambivalent – as the beauty of the mermaid with legs, but no voice, is insufficient enticement for the prince to marry her – so while the theme of the present work is that the history of Sirens is one where sound is not enough – in Andersen's story, the body is equally not enough. Andersen informs the reader that the prince had never thought of marrying the mermaid. In the tale the mermaid has an opportunity to return to the sea a mermaid, but only if she kills the prince which she refuses to do – thus consigning her to a soulless existence partially redeemed at the end of the tale, due to her 'goodness'. Both Kafka's and Hans Christian Andersen's Sirens are silenced – a joining of modernism and the popular in the literary imagination.

11

Sonic Aftermaths

Sirens and Stormy Daniels

The large, gaudy neon light shines brightly in Columbus, Ohio, America's fourteenth-largest but fastest-growing city – the Sirens Gentleman's Club, its sign, appears incongruously polite, genteel and arcane as it lights up the treeless car park before enticing its 'gentlemen' clientele to its doors. Adjacent to the club is a motorway, cars streaming past in the evening hours, in front a large car park. There are no trees or vegetation; it is a sombre, utilitarian scene. The club's webpage shows a 1970s single-storey building, a restaurant in a previous incarnation. The allure of this 'land locked' neon Siren sign is known in contemporary America and elsewhere. The person the audience have come to see, Stormy Daniels, is dubbed 'the President's Personal Porn Star' on the club's neon lighting and is also the director of many pornographic movies in which she frequently stars (Daniels 2018). These 'gentlemen' driving into the parking lot bear little relationship to Homer's Odysseus – they are not travelling home by sea to their families after performing death-defying feats. Theirs is a more mundane 'adventure'. The club is a 'strip club' where the clientele watch topless women dance before them while they look, eat, drink or perhaps talk with other men or even their wives or girlfriends. The club briefly shot to international prominence with the arrest of Stormy Daniels on the evening of 11 July 2018. The audience, fuller than normal and more diverse than the middle-aged white men who were its regular clientele, had come to see Daniels, not perhaps for her professional fame but because of her well-publicized dispute with the American president concerning the status of a non-disclosure agreement (NDA) that she had signed concerning a sexual liaison she had had with the president before he ran for office. In this instance, and in many other instances, NDAs are signed in order to silence one party and protect the other. The *MeToo* movement recently commented upon the number of such agreements signed by actresses who allegedly had been sexually assaulted by movie moguls. Daniels had fully agreed to her liaison with the would-be American president, with the NDA serving to cover up embarrassment rather than wrongdoing. Silencing the preferred outcome.

The purpose of this trace – the contingent naming of the Sirens Gentleman's Club; many such establishments, after all, have different names while providing the same 'service'. Yet the cultural trace remains. Daniels, the object of attraction, does not sing like the original Sirens – hers is a bodily attraction embodied in the myth from Apollonius onwards as is her silencing, culturally, legally and interpersonally. That Daniels had strived to regain her legal voice became part of the attraction for audiences. Daniels remained silenced as she danced, like Kafka's Sirens, in silence – but with rhythmic backing music (recorded, not live) – no sound emitting from her mouth; unlike Kafka's Sirens she had no desire for her clientele – she was merely performing as her profession expects, mechanically (Daniels 2018). A twenty-first century Tiller Girl fully commodified (Kracauer 1995) in parallel time to Kafka's Sirens described by Dolar as – automations – going through the motions – cyborg like (Dolar 2006). The voice giving way to the body as a symbol of desire as in so much of popular culture, mediated in film, computer games-distant, yet present. The desire for the Siren in this instance – a fully embodied and physically present Stormy Daniels – was coming from the audience – some of whom touched Daniels's exposed breasts while she danced. Undercover police present in the club arrested Daniels, not the perpetrators of the 'offence'. There is film of Daniels being escorted from the club and placed in a police van. A photograph shows Daniels, clothed yet handcuffed, dazed as she looks into the camera from the back of a police van on her way to be transported to court and jail. Minutes before, she had been the centre of attention to an adoring and expectant audience. As the police van moves off, it uses its police siren to speed its way through the suburban highways of Columbus, Ohio. A confluence of the ideology of mythical Sirens laid bare with the material sirens protecting whom and from what?

On arrival at the Columbus police station Daniels is charged, according to online court records, with three misdemeanour counts of touching a patron at a 'sexually oriented' business in violation of an Ohio strip club law. The police report accused her of touching 'a specified anatomical area' of individuals who were present at the performance, including, ironically, the undercover police officers who had reported the incident. The following morning Daniels left the police station after having had all charges against her dropped – the supposed victim of a police sting operation. Daniel's attorney had claimed at the hearing that undercover police officers had asked Daniels for permission to place their faces between her breasts.

In the *Odyssey* it is the Siren voice which is described as deadly to the men who listen. Three thousand years later in Columbus, Ohio, it is the voiceless Siren who suffers the consequences of physical contact with those who merely look. The Siren holds no danger to the paying customers of the Sirens Gentleman's Club. Stormy Daniels, a mover in the porn industry, is herself, perhaps, an anachronism. Twenty-first-century Sirens are more likely to resemble the 'cyborgs' of film and computer games but now made from synthetic 'flesh' representing a new Siren domesticity. The sex industry has recently developed $15,000 life-sized silicone dolls that talk, laugh and smile and which their owners can engage in sexual acts with. Truly Sirens for the twenty-first century?

12

Sonic Fallibility

Kittler's Sirens

> *The element of semi-erudition shows itself in the failure of the mind to recognise the fallacy not of the material thus interconnected, but of the spuriousness of the link.*
>
> (ADORNO 2005A: 119)

The sea is calm on this April day in 2004, the yacht moves slowly through the early spring waters off the Li Galli islands in the bay of Salerno. Aboard the yacht is the famous German media theorist Frederik Kittler – the sea is quiet, much like it must have been 3,000 years earlier when Homer imagined Odysseus's temptation on hearing the song of the Sirens. On this day it was not the Sirens of myth who sang but three female singers from the German National Opera – standing atop the rocks singing as loudly as they could as Kittler's yacht sailed slowly past. Kittler, disappointed, could not hear the singing of the opera singers. Maybe Kittler had not fully understood the contingent nature of voice and space across the ocean. The propagation of sound is variable, dependent upon a range of atmospheric conditions. The use of foghorns, for example, were only variably effective at sea, albeit in weather conditions less advantageous than those Kittler was experiencing – a sound originating 45 degrees to the right or 30 degrees to the left, in fog, cannot necessarily be determined just as it is difficult to ascertain the distance of the sonic warning.[1]

Frederik Kittler had taken a team of researchers from Humboldt University to investigate the sonic archaeology of the Li Galli islands. The aims of the project appeared to be twofold – to scientifically test the soundscape for evidence of their potential material ground for the provenance of the Siren myth. As Wolfgang Ernst has observed, the expedition 'measured the sonosphere of the acoustic theatre where the Homeric Sirens are supposed to have sung, resulting in surprising findings about the acoustic reality lurking behind the myth' (Ernst 2014: 7). In parallel to this, Kittler was also interested in testing the 'literal' nature of the myth by placing opera singers atop the islands in order that they might sing 'like' the Sirens.

The Siren voices, as has been noted earlier, are not embodied in Homer but rather provide an early example of acousmatic sound. The tale can be construed as one of technological intervention – of wax placed in the ears of Odysseus's crew so that only Odysseus hears – and is tempted by the Siren's singing.[2] In the historical interpretation of the text, reinvented, clawed over endlessly from Plato to Kafka, from Ovid to Sloterdijk, from H. G. Wells to the directors of endless Hollywood Siren movies; the history of Sirens from both a cultural and a theoretical perspective illustrates the point that the sonic has been insufficient as an explanatory trope as Sirens metamorphose into half-birds, half-women, mermaids, femme-fatales or indeed *all* women – fully embodied and visualized.[3] To *see* the Sirens, so history informs us, is to succumb to temptation – this temptation is the sole reserve of men and is misogynistic from beginning to end.[4] Women in the many historical accounts of Sirens rarely hear them or if they do they remain *untouched* by their song whether that song's desire be embedded in the hearer's desire for knowledge, flesh or aesthetics.[5] If Odysseus had been able to both *hear* and *see* the Sirens – the wax would become redundant with the crew, being able to see but not hear, rebelling and, infused with physical desire would have rowed to the shore to willingly embrace their slow destruction. One might have thought that Kittler would have focused upon the acousmatic nature of the Siren episode in his media archaeology in order to understand the Sirens as an early precursor to the sonic in the age of mechanical reproduction as a precursor to the disembodied voice of the telephone, the radio and the record player; infusing contemporary culture with a sonic nostalgia, for a sonic life after death embodied in a range of technologically inspired aspirations – desires embodied in the early-twentieth-century psycho-phone and other technologically mediated experiences (Schmidt 2000; Sconce 2000). But no, Kittler enamoured by the power of the Sirens song puts opera singers on top of the Li Galli cliffs – a literal, embodied exercise in Siren experience.

What indeed were the wider aspirations of the research teams in going to the Li Galli islands? Homer's writing of the *Odyssey* appears intimately related to the geography of travel and trade in the Greece of the time. Indeed, the proclivity of the Sirens to both attract and destroy male sailors have often been attributed to the dangers of life at sea of the time. In Homer's account, the Sirens, whatever they may have been, appeared to reside on land, not the ocean.[6] Wolfgang Ernst argues that the significance of the Li Galli islands in relation to the Homeric myth is that a media archaeological investigation might well suggest that the Siren sounds were merely natural sounds emanating from the geography of the Li Galli islands that fed into the myth. The literalness of Kittler's use of opera singers sits strangely next to the more 'scientific' nature of the research project aimed at tracing the potential materiality of the myth – as a successful example of what a media archaeology might achieve.[7] The search for a 'materiality' underlying the Homeric myth is not, however, new; it goes back almost as far as the myth itself and is embodied in the social thought of Aristotle and Epicurus all the way through to the contemporary practices of media archaeology under scrutiny here. Ernst poses the epistemological and methodological question well when he writes 'any media archaeology of past acoustics has to confront the dilemma. How can a sonic event which is supposed to have happened long before the age of gramophonic recording be verified' (Ernst 2014). The question of sonic materiality within the Siren episode translates into a simple proposition: Could sailors have mistaken the natural sounds of rock, wind and sea for the sounds of the Sirens? This proposition itself is based upon the reasonable assumption that the *Odyssey* itself could have been based on the shipping routes used by Greek sailors of antiquity. If so, could not a materiality be at the core of the myth – at least as far as the Sirens episode is concerned? All that is required is to ascertain which island or shoreline might produce sounds that might be taken to be Siren sounds. This question is then developed into asking could the sounds of the Li Galli islands be mistaken for Sirenic voices and could this experience be translated into the literary, albeit male, imagination of Homer and others? Whether it is justified to abstract out the Siren episode from the other adventures of Odysseus which include sonic experience around specific places is a moot point, but is an example with a rich history in Siren cultural representation. Ernst cites early geographical writings as justification for locating the Siren episode in the Li Galli islands, 'The media-archaeological investigation performed on the site of the Li Galli islands provided evidence that the myth – which since Strabon's *Geographica* has been sure about the location – "echoes" actual acoustic phenomena on the site. For such a precise location of cultural memory, there must be a foundation in the acoustic real' (Ernst 2014: 9).

The notion that there 'must' be a material 'foundation' to the myth, and that this 'materiality' lies in the Li Galli islands is problematic. The desire to investigate the connection itself appears to demand a surprising suspension of critical and methodological judgement – representing an incipient teleology of thought. The location of the Li Galli islands as the material base of the myth is at best contentious, as Emily Wilson, the first and only female translator of the *Odyssey* argues,

> The geographical setting of the Odyssey is almost as hard to pin down as its temporal location. Some of the places visited by Odysseus are obviously fictional or mythical – the Land of the Dead, the island of the Sirens, the home of the monster Scylla and the whirlpool Charybdis, or the city of the giant, cannibalistic Laestrygonians ... the poem has little interest in the realistic depiction of geography. (Wilson 2017: 16)

Kittler's research team studiously went forth laying sophisticated and multiple recording technologies along the Li Galli islands in search of the elusive 'Siren' sounds that were thought to be produced by the physicality of the islands. The success of their endeavours was such that members of the research team wrote: 'Our results support the hypothesis that the song of the Sirens in Homer's epic is based upon a real acoustic event at Li Galli. ... The quest, however, of what kinds of beings or what exactly emitted the extolled sirenic sounds among the Li Galli islands cannot be decided on the basis of currently obtained measurements' (Frommholt and Carle 2014:

29). Accepting this premise, we might well ask for comparative sonic experiments to be undertaken elsewhere in order to test the hypothesis – it is unclear from the results as to which material sounds of nature would sound like the following,

> Odysseus! Come here! You are well known
> From many stories! Glory to the Greeks!
> Now stop your ship and listen to our voices.
> All those who pass this way hear honeyed song,
> Poured from our mouths. (Odyssey 2017)

Yet the very belief in the materiality behind the Homeric myth is based on traces of literature and historical accounts that themselves buy into the myth rather than question it. The use of sophisticated technological equipment to measure the sound of the islands merely compounds the error rather than demonstrating the materiality of the myth. The contention that the myth was based, in some sense, upon literal geographical space rather than on imaginary space propelled Kittler and his team to believe that the Li Galli islands are indeed the probable location for either the origin of the myth or indeed the 'truth' of the myth. These assumptions concerning the location of Homeric places existed in ancient Greek and Roman writings. The Old Testament placed the home of the Sirens in Babylon, interestingly not on water:

> Now the beasts make their homes there
> And an empty echo is heard in the houses
> Sirens have their habitation there
> And demons dance.
> Onocentaurs dwell there
> And hedgehogs breed in the halls. (Isa. 13.21-22)

Equally, the dualism inherent in Kittler's Odyssey experiments – scientific and literal – were prefigured by the tenth-century writer Guido of Arezzo who surmised that Sirenic sounds might be attributed to the sound of the rocks on the shore or equally to the voices of Sirens that lure sailors to their stony deaths:

> They say that the sirens are songstresses of the sea, who kill incautious sailors whom they have attracted to themselves by

especially sweet melodies. There are some hollow rocks jutting out of the sea, on which the clash of the storm-winds imitates sweet-sounding melody. When it attracts passing sailors with its sweetness, it sometimes sinks them in pitiful shipwreck, just as the flattering Sirens of this world, namely its attractions, sink those like ourselves in the most perilous shipwreck of their souls. (in Leach 2006: 198)

Both Kittler and Ernst think that the evidence for Li Galli being the physical source of the myth is overwhelming. Tom McCarthy who interviewed Kittler claimed that he informed him that 'the Li Galli rocks were literally "where" the Sirens sung from "placed on the very rocks on which Homer located them (these can be identified with total accuracy, he assured me.)"' (McCarthy 2011). Strabo cited by Ernst as providing early proof of the location of the Sirens is instructive. Strabo, a renowned Roman geographer of the first century might be interpreted as a staunch defender of the Homeric tale in sceptical times. During that period within Rome, Homer had been the subject of 'empirical' contestation by Lucretius and others. Strabo's work represented a defence of Homeric writing at the time through his attempt at providing 'physical' evidence of the sites of the Homeric myth – thereby claiming their 'veracity' was grounded in empirical 'fact'. Strabo's work might be understood as an early Roman example of advocacy. Yet Kahles argues that Strabo believed that *all* of Homer's tales were based upon 'real' history – not *just* the Siren episode but the monster Scylla, the whirlpool Charybdis and so on:

Aeolus was once the king over the islands of Liparaei. The Cyclopes and the Laestrygonians were lords over the region about Aetna and Leontini, and for this reason the Strait was avoided, and Scylla and Charybdis were infested with brigands. In the same way we find that the rest of the people mentioned by Homer lived in other parts of the world. (Kahles 1976: 25)

Strabo himself argued for a level of caution concerning the precise physical locations of Homer's myths stating that 'we do not seek that the poet be absolutely accurate in every detail. Even so we are not able to assume that Homer put together the story of Odysseus' wanderings without any knowledge at all of how they took place'. (Strabo 2014: 29)

Kittler's own interest in and knowledge of Strabo's claims appear to derive from more recent sources such as Ernie Branford's writings on the Siren episode of the *Odyssey* which in turn was derived from Norman Douglas's earlier work *Siren Land* written in 1911 at the tail end of the Victorian obsession with Sirens and indeed mermaids. Both reference the work of Strabo as 'proving' the placing of the Homeric Sirens:

> Strabo, the Latin poets, and many classical writers place the Sirens unhesitatingly somewhere in the region of the Gulf of Naples. This makes good sense geographically, for Ulysses will have followed the coast of Italy southward as far as possible, whichever route he intended to take home. Any sailing instructions will have enumerated the islands which the mariner must pass before making. ... Capri has been claimed by some as the home of the Sirens, but the general opinion of classical writers was that the Siren islands should be identified with Galli islets, which lie at the entrance to the Gulf of Salerno. (Douglas 2010: 120)

Douglas devotes two chapters of *Siren Land* in his description of the Li Galli islands and their caves. While Branford's interest in the Sirens is not the same as the Humbolt University's research team, it does appear to marry up with Frederik Kittlers'. Kittler appeared to have been impressed with Bradford's claim to have heard the Sirens off the coast of Li Galli in the Second World War. It is worth describing Bradford's account in some detail:

> The music crept by me upon the waters. ... I heard them sounding like singing. I cannot describe it accurately, but it was low and somehow distant – a 'natural' kind of singing one might call it, reminiscent of the waves and the wind. Yet it was certainly neither of these, for there was about it a human quality, disturbing and evocative.
>
> How could I hear a low singing aboard a ship? The answer is that most of the time we were patrolling very slowly, and then stopping altogether for long periods. It was during one of these periods when we were stopped and I heard the singing. ... On the next leg of our patrol when we were close by the rocks and

stopped again, I listened carefully. I heard it again, but much nearer, so it seemed – and now for some unaccountable reason I felt afraid.

I nudged Nobby, and asked him if he could hear anything. 'No', he said. 'Nothing at all.' Even as he spoke I could hear the singing – it wasn't one voice but several. I could not make out any words, nor any particular tune. ... Somehow or other I knew that it was feminine, for no man's throat could have made that low, sweet noise ... so we stopped there – and none of the others could hear it. Neither the Captain, nor Nobby Clarke, my watchmate, nor any of the bridge lookouts. 'You're going round the bend', Nobby murmured. (Bradford 2004: 132–3)

Bradford discounts the Siren sounds as anything other than 'feminine' – his account is one of 'close listening', aware of the listening condition as interrupted by the ships motor – he hears the Sirens when the ships motor is at rest. Importantly Bradford recognizes that only he hears the Sirens, nobody else on board the ship hears them – even after he has informed them that he is hearing 'voices' out at sea or from the Li Galli islands themselves. On returning to the islands on his yacht after the Second World War, in search of the Sirens song, and in the company of his wife he fails to hear the Sirens stating that:

Perhaps the reason why I never heard them on my second visit was that I had my wife with me. There is no record of the Sirens ever having sung to a ship that had a woman on board. However old the Sirens may be, and however deep their knowledge of all that passes on this earth and of all that shall ever be, they are still women. They do not want anything from their own sex. (Bradford 2004: 134)

Geoffrey Winthrop-Young rightly points out the gendered assumption concerning the Sirens that Bradford makes – that Sirens are only interested in men – or by implication that women are not interested in Sirens so hence, paradoxically, cannot hear them. However, it is important to note the parallel point, that it is only Bradford who hears the Sirens on-board his ship, none of the other male crew members hear anything. This solo act of 'hearing' appears to place Bradford in the shoes of Odysseus himself while the other crew members are akin to Homers' rowers albeit without the technology of the wax in their ears to account for their non-hearing. In his act of solo hearing Bradford becomes a 'superior' listener. The importance attributed to the notion of the superior listener, in contrast to the seductive nature of the voice itself, has its origins in the Middle Ages which at times emphasized the morality of the listener rather than that of the singer: 'Thus, the authority of true judgement is undermined and taken away from the ears that listen to them, and the heart, which the melody of such great sweetness thus delights and ravishes, does not suffer to examine properly the merits of the song that it hears' (John Clanvowe quoted in Leach 2006: 189).

For Clanvowe and others, the ability to both discern and then reject the Siren voices was an issue of 'morality' rather than merely of hearing. Sloterdijk also claims, in relation to the Siren's song, that each listener hears their own song:

> To hear them is to recognise that one's transformation into song is complete and one's life goal thus attained. ... Whoever hears such songs of himself can assume that his own life is now a serious topic of conversation at the table of the Gods. This then is why siren rock becomes the cliff on which the prematurely honoured perish. There is no path leading back to the everyday, unsung existence from the grave song in their own lifetime. (Sloterdijk 2011: 496)

Branford does not share this fate, he was not lured onto the rocks, neither did he jump overboard like the hapless sailor in *Jason and the Argonauts*. Bradford's tale highlights the consistent meaning attributed to the Sirens over millennia, its gendered nature and its orientation around the nature of male desire, as against the geographical location of the myth which is only partial. Indeed, the mermaids of the nineteenth and twentieth centuries appear to traverse the oceans of the world in search of their 'male' prey. Kittler's interest in the Sirens appears to fulfil all three criteria. When discussing his inability to hear the German opera singers imitating Homer's Sirens, with Tom McCarthy he commented that it meant, 'that Homer was deliberately setting a false trail: what he's telling us between the lines is that Odysseus disembarked, swam to the rocks and fucked the Sirens' (McCarthy: 2). Kittler, Bradford and others merely represent a continuation of the gender stereotyping embedded in the Siren myth. Kittler's 'Arcadian hardcore porn' is alive and well in popular culture and in parts of academia. Given the brilliance of Kittler's own *Gramophone, Film, Typewriter* (1999) it is surprising that he felt it necessary to visit the Li Galli islands at all – rather than merely returning to the myth and decode its meaning for its sonic archaeology. As Odysseus blocks the ears of his crew with wax and waits to hear the sounds of the Sirens. Strapped to the mast of his ship – ears open – the space of audition paradoxically becomes a space for Odysseus and the Sirens alone – the first example of a technological privatizing of space, intimate, immediate and exclusionary. As Odysseus listens, the space between him and the Sirens is a precursor to Walkman and iPod users as they commune with the sonic products of the culture industry – an acousmatic experience of the twentieth and twenty-first centuries – an audiovisual experience as they look out onto the world with their very own 'personalized' soundtrack – an experience of intense pleasure without the pitfalls of succumbing to the Sirens (Bull 2000, 2007).

Postscript: Kittler's Mast of the Imagination

But let's not end there. There is also something profoundly heroic about Frederik Kittler's Siren folly. After all, aren't all Siren encounters a folly of some description? Let us imagine Kittler tied to the mast of his own imagination as his ship lies off the coast of the Li Galli islands. Like Kafka's Sirens – Kittler hears no sound – stretching his neck until the islands recede. In his head, he hears, not the Sirens but rather, the strains of Pink Floyd's *Dark Side of the Moon*.[8] Kittler has already described the ecstatic nature of listening to Pink Floyd whereby their singing voices

> implode in our ears. ... As if there were no distance between the recorded voice and listening ears, as if voices travelled along the transmitting bones of self-perception directly from the mouth into the ear's labrynth, hallucinations become real. (Kittler1999: 37)

As we imagine Kittler listening to the soaring wordless voice of Claire Torry in *The Great Gig in the Sky* ending with the voice of Roger Waters in *Eclipse* intoning:

> And everything under the sun is in tune
> But the sun is eclipsed by the moon.

One imagines Kittler, tied to the mast, replaying in his imagination the soundtrack, as on a Walkman, recursively. And as he experiences the silence in between the end of, and the rewinding of, and the playing of the album anew – like Sisyphus – one must imagine him happy.[9]

Afterword: Let's Sing Another Song Boys. This One Has Grown Old and Bitter (Leonard Cohen)

> *The mortification of the flesh by power was nothing other than the ideological reflection of the oppression practiced on them.*
>
> (HORKHEIMER AND ADORNO)

Mermaids are more popular than Sirens in contemporary culture. Mermaid parades exist from Lee-On-Sea in the UK to California, Michigan and countless other cities. These parades appear good natured, inclusive and well attended. The South Haven Mermaid Parade online marketing announces: 'There are many other fun activities throughout the entire weekend for old and young alike. And it's not just for mermaids – mermen and merkids, along with sailors and nefarious pirates, will be everywhere! Fun for the whole family'.

The main event is however the parade and participants are requested to make their own mermaid costume, the website shows women from previous parades displaying their costumes, posing in groups before the camera. Many other parades appear as outlets for the professional making and selling of mermaid costumes with contestants able to take lessons on how to swim safely with their fishtail costumes as Annette Kellermann had done in silent cinema 100 years ago. The contestants have probably never heard of Kellermann, indeed she is largely forgotten, ironic, as she invented the single female swimsuit that women wear today enabling them to swim unencumbered by the then voluminous, constraining, yet 'modest' swimwear of the time. These parades owe more to Disney that to Homer. The title *Sirens* is sometimes used by the LGBT community as in the Siren World Pride March in New York City in 2019 to perhaps indicate a metamorphosis of sexual identity and as such its political meaning differs from the popular culture of the mermaid parades. Elsewhere the term might denote a female-only musical group as with the *Siren Baroque*, an all-female baroque ensemble based in New York. The mermaid parades are 'harmless' commodified fun while the LGBT use of the term has potentially more radical political connotations. The question remains: Can a repressive 'male' category of Sirens and mermaids be successfully re-appropriated by women themselves? Dijkstra in her sweeping analysis of misogyny within cultural practices of fin-de-siècle culture thought possibly so arguing that female sea creatures appeared as stronger, more passionate and freer than the highly restricted roles that women of the time were obliged to play:

> No wonder that many turn-of-the-century women were attracted to such paintings as that of Whiteley, and to the ambiguous image of the liberated female which they represented, for these women must have thought that it was better to be feared as a predator than to be distained as a fool. In fact, it is clear that in their imaginative sweep, paintings such as Whiteley's obliquely paid tribute to the world of the New Woman. (Dijkstra 1986: 265)

> Austern and Naroditskaya concur when they point to a shift in the latter stages of the nineteenth century whereby 'women came to re-claim her [the Siren] as their heritage. Women's re-appropriation of the male-created Siren increased steadily throughout both centuries, perhaps as part of the global reclamation of femininity from male dominance'. (Austern and Naroditskaya 2006: 10)

Yet these assertions of 'freedom' embodied in the negative male category existed side by side with unprecedented levels of male dominance and violence towards women both in daily life and articulated in the artistic products of the time as this volume has articulated through many of its cultural traces.

Adorno's position on this appears ambivalent, the quote with which this trace begins appears to suggest not, one cannot make a virtue from the marks of oppression bodily or cognitively or through counter ideology – that these marks are the result of male ideology do not make them any less 'real'. Adorno, himself, never seems to have recovered from an incident in one of his 1960s lectures in Frankfurt when two female students stripped off proclaiming that this, their bodies, were the meaning of the cultural revolution. Herbert Marcuse, unusually, appears to support Adorno in his critique of elements of the cultural revolution of the time which he argued were themselves commodified arguing that the reclaiming of repressive male imagery – woman as body, as nature, as sex object – rather than liberatory was merely a form of 'repressive desublimation' whereby the 'object' of repression becomes magically transformed into a 'vehicle' of liberation.

Elsewhere in the *Dialectic of Enlightenment* Adorno's understanding of the 'natural', a core element in his dialectic appears problematic in his discussion of the dialectics relationship to women. His work has recently been the subject of sympathetic feminist critiques: 'Adorno is engaged in representing the degraded situation of women in heteropatriarchal society, rather than endorsing it' (Duford 2017: 785). Rochelle Duford argues that Adorno demonstrates the ways in which women in 'seeming to represent untamed nature shows the ways in which conceptually she has been constructed as artifice through structures and systems of domination' (Duford 2017: 788). However Andrew Hewitt points to the apparent silencing of women in the *Dialectic of Enlightenment* as resulting from their very instrumentalization arguing that, 'to assert that the domination of woman is the domination of nature is to accept at some level – the very process of identification [of woman as nature] which serves to dominate' (Hewitt 1992: 153). If this interpretation is correct, then Adorno falls victim to his own mythical notion of 'nature'. Yet Lillian Doherty takes a different position concerning the relationship between nature and culture in the *Odyssey*:

> [The Odyssey], evokes images of ostensible female power that in fact serve to reinforce a male dominated gender system. But it is equally important for female readers to locate images that can elude or subvert this kind of co-option. I see the Homeric sirens as one such image, precisely because in contrast to the Muses they are unaligned with any male authority, human or

divine. They are potentially sexual, but narrative, not sex, is the true source of their power. Thus they can elude the assimilation of femaleness to 'nature' and sexuality, for their language is impeccably that of culture. (Doherty in Cohen 1995: 88)

This trace began with a reference to the star of silent movies, Annette Kellermann, now almost forgotten and I wonder what Franz Kafka, silent cinema enthusiast, would have made of her as he wrote 'The Silence of the Sirens', the subject of a previous trace, fearful and desirous perhaps, her movies were not shown in Prague, Kafka's home. Kellermann might have been silent on the screen but not as a cultural presence. So how does Annette Kellermann feature in the repressive or progressive divide within the presentation of sirens within culture?

The Sirens of cinema do not begin with Walt Disney – but well before that in the era of silent cinema, the first representations of Sirens, or rather 'mermaids' all featured the competitive swimmer, athlete, inventor of the first women's one-piece swimsuit and indeed the first woman to appear naked in a Hollywood movie – Annette Kellermann. She was described by the media of the time as 'the perfect woman' and as a 'real-life mermaid'. She performed in, and co-wrote *Siren of the Sea* (1911), *The Mermaids* (1911), *Neptune's Daughter* (1914), *A Daughter of the Gods* (1916) and *Queen of the Sea* (1918). In these films Kellermann's mermaid emphasized the exotic and the 'primitive'. She was always filmed doing her own stunts included filming many scenes underwater. As Philip Hayward noted, the filming of Kellermann resulted, 'in a significant spectacularisation of her body ... that constructed her as an impossible object of desire' (Hayward 2018: 174). Hayward also points to her 'paradoxical' social position of the time, 'changing social patterns allowed and enabled her to become famous for her physical accomplishments in terms usually reserved for male performances. But at the same time, her various appearances as a mermaid also served to represent her as essentially pre-modern and elemental' (Hayward 2108: 174). Kellermann was no Hans Christian Andersen 'mermaid' – but rather an adventurous swashbuckling heroine – albeit 'exoticized'. While Kellermann's body was a subject of much public debate she also acted as a representative for 'emancipated' women as she swam across the English channel, liberated women from traditional swimwear thus permitting them to swim as 'men' and wrote and co-directed many of her films. Yet her fame was prefaced on her appearance as a mermaid?

> After seeing her one may feel like defying any ten foot man in the audience to declare that the sex of which she is an ideal example hasn't the courage to fight or the ability to vote or do anything else they choose to do. If votes were obtained by physical or mental courage, Miss Kellermann would demand a million of them. (*Boston Post* in Gibson 2005: 149)

Kellermann, an early-twentieth-century feminist, portrays the ambivalence attached to using problematic male stereotypes such as the mermaid or siren. The question remains, are Sirens or Mermaids worthy of re-appropriation in the twenty-first century – or should we sing another song 'boys'?

NOTES

Sounding Out the Sirens

1 Throughout the text I use the capital 'S' for Sirens of myth and the lower case 's' to denote all other examples of sirens. When discussing both, I use the rather clumsy 'Sirens/sirens' if appropriate, or more generally the lower case 's' as a generic term.

2 The French scientist Cagniard de la Tour is credited with inventing the first 'siren' in 1819, calling his invention a siren due to his fascination with Greek myth and that his invention could emit sound underwater and above ground as he imagined mythical Sirens could.

3 Theodor Adorno and Max Horkheimer in their 1947 classic *Dialectic of Enlightenment* render a provocative reading of Homer's Sirens – but air-raid sirens? Their literal use of 'sirens' only occurs once, in their description of Hitler's use of the radio, in which the term 'siren' is used as an adjective. The present work moves beyond any merely literal use of the term to investigate the threads connecting sirens to broader social and political explanations of their meaning and use.

4 In 1970, as a young teenager I bought a copy of Tim Buckley's *Starsailor*, a record I still possess, but now rarely play. As a young man I was particularly drawn to his beautiful and, for me, enigmatic 'Siren Song', the shortest yet most beautiful of all of the tracks. I had no significant knowledge of Sirens at the time and hadn't read Homer's *Odyssey*, but it appealed to a melancholic adolescent understanding of romance. The lyrics conform largely to the Homeric myth:

> Long afloat on shipless oceans
> I did all my best to smile
> ... O my heart, O my heart shies from the sorrow

The lyrics, sung by Buckley, are a dialogue between Buckley as Odysseus and the Sirens, evoking the draw of the Sirens both visually and sonically. The Siren (there is only one) does not sing of knowledge, but of desire: 'Let me enfold you'. Buckley's lyrics are ambiguous as to who is chasing whom: 'Were you hare when I was fox?' As the ship sinks the Siren replies that she is not for touching and he is to return tomorrow – but we discover that the song was merely a dream. The song has struck a chord with other musicians, inspiring forty-seven cover versions, the majority of them recent. Most impressive is the 2017 cover by Wolf Alice, who captures the song's melancholy from the perspective of the Siren.

5 The use of the term 'trace' is an adaptation from Bloch's method of writing in *Traces* (2006) – adapted in so far as Bloch often begins his trace from a childhood experience before extending his observation, tracing it through a wide range of cultural experiences and examples. The present work often starts each trace with an illustrative cultural, historical or theoretical observation rather than with a biographical one – with one or two exceptions. In reviewing Bloch's work Korstvedt describes the method as 'to stimulate an imaginatively critical, questioning, even questing, attitude that can read clues and signs from ordinary lived experience in ways that reveal the mutually determining relationship between existential and social being' (Korstvedt 2007). Adorno, in a nuanced critique of Bloch, describes his use of the method in the following terms: 'These experiences are no more esoteric than whatever it was about the sound of Christmas bells which moved us so profoundly and which we never wholly outgrow: the feeling that this can't be all, that there must be something more than just the here and now' (Adorno 1980).

6 A note on the name, Odysseus is the original Greek name. At times the name Ulysses is also used, this refers to the Latin or English translation of the name. Odysseus is used in the present book unless specific authors have used Ulysses – for example, James Joyce's book *Ulysses*.

Chapter 1

1 Kurt Vonnegut, who experienced the bombing of Dresden, placed the number of deaths that night at 115,000. This figure has been whittled down till, in 2008, a new, much lower figure was suggested, 'After four years' work, an impressive commission of German historians this week filed its report on this issue, and it seems that even the lowest figure so far accepted may be an overestimate. Drawing on archival sources, many never previously consulted, on burial records and scientific findings – including street-by-street archaeological investigations – plus hundreds of eye-witness reports, the Dresden Commission of Historians for the Ascertainment of the Number of Victims of

the Air Raids on the City of Dresden on 13/14 February 1945 has provisionally estimated the likely death-toll at around 18,000 and definitely no more than 25,000'. 'How Many Died in the Bombing of Dresden?' Frederick Taylor, Speigel Online, 2 October 2008.

2 The term 'Sirens' is used generically to refer to all mythical creatures of the sea following the French use of the term 'Sirenes.' 'Siren, mermaid, femme fatale – the linguistic distinction doesn't exist in French where all water women, whether friendly or dangerous are referred to as Sirenes' (Euchner 2012: 39).

Chapter 2

1 Wilson (2017) argues that while Homeric tales would have started life as oral tales, the length and sophistication of the *Odyssey* would have precluded both the memorizing of the text and the ability of listeners to follow for such a lengthy renditioning of the poem. This results from a qualitatively different *Odyssey* from whatever came before it orally.

Chapter 3

1 The discussion as to any potential 're-voicing' of Sirens from a feminist perspective is undertaken in chapter 12.

2 That these sonic and often visual representations of Sirens/women conformed to the dominant male binary ideology is commented upon by Euchner in her discussion of Wagner's Rhinemaidens and of women in general to the social thought dominant at the time: 'By making herself the means for man's satisfaction, woman gives up her personality; she only gets it, and her whole dignity back by having done it out of love for that one man. ... She has ceased to live life as an individual; her life has become part of his life' (Fichte in Euchner 2012: 47).

3 In Iraq in 2005, the favoured music among the troops was metal and rap played through iPods and loudspeakers – Metallica's , 'One' a favourite, 'about a fictional World War I soldier, who is injured in an attack and loses his arms, legs, and the ability to see, hear, smell, and taste' (Pieslak 2009: 148). Tony Lagouranis, an army interrogator in Iraq, describes interrogation methods that he and others undertook in Iraq:

> The music, such as it was, consisted of industrial style guitars, beating drums, and lyrics delivered in a moan/shout style, the

singer obviously trying to sound like the Prince of Darkness himself. It blasted out of the speakers and ricocheted around the container. Even though his head was bagged, we knew Umar could see the light flashing, even if his eyes were closed. I knew because I tried it myself. ... And as Umar knelt, we took turns at yelling our questions into his ears. His head twisted around as he tried to figure out where we were. After about half an hour, he started moaning. I imagined he was crying behind his sandbag. ... As we moved into our second hour of this treatment, Umar still on his knees, Evan and I were jolted by a huge boom and a series of screams outside the container. It took a second to register that it was someone – no, a bunch of people – banging the container walls and yelling at the top of their voices. Someone was hitting the outside with a rifle butt or a piece of lumber, someone else was whooping, 'Yee haa.' Some soldiers obviously heard the music, figured out what was going on, and decided to join the party. (Lagouranis 2007: 116)

A fitting testimony of the use of music as torture, and, as with Homer's Sirens, there is no need to touch the victim.

Chapter 4

1 The twentieth century saw an unprecedented development of sophisticated unmanned 'death at a distance' technologies. The first of these, the V2 flying missile was responsible for countless 'invisible' deaths on the south coast of England in 1943. The confluence between film and destruction so common in communication technologies of the twentieth century is demonstrated in 1930 when Braun the German rocket scientist went to a Berlin cinema to see the Fritz Lang movie *Women on the Moon* – the mock rocket having been designed by his friend Herman Oberth. Braun was so taken with the film that he had the film's rocket logo painted on the first V2 bomb to be dropped onto London.

2 Paris, like many other European cities, has retained its Second World War air-raid sirens. Practice soundings are undertaken on the first Wednesday of each month at 12.00 and 12.10 p.m. The sirens sound for forty seconds on each occasion. Max Neuhaus has commented on the problems of locating the whereabouts of police sirens, writing, 'It turns out these sounds have many problems, the major one being that they are almost impossible to locate. Universally people say that they cannot tell where a siren sound is coming from until it is

upon them. Unable to find the sound and becoming more nervous by its approach, many drivers simply stop and block traffic until they figure out what to do. Others ignore the sound until they are directly confronted by the vehicle, sometimes with lethal results' (Neuhaus 1993).

3 Frank Reniere recalls what air raids in Brussels during the Second World War sounded like: 'At first, it had been like some sort of annoying ritual to have to get down to the cellar, but after a while I realized this was a reaction to a very real danger of having the whole building falling on our heads. ... It took me several years after the war to get out of the habit, when planes were overhead, of ducking and looking for a nearby shelter. Sirens are sounded for checks every first Thursday of the month at noon and even now, more than sixty years later, I still can't suppress the millisecond burst of some deep-planted feeling of fear' ('A Young Boy and the Good War', accessed 16 June 2016, https:WWII-netherlands-escape-lines.com/personal-narratives/a-young-boy-and-the-good-war-2).

4 Barrington Moore Jr. argued that human misery was a more uniform category than the diversity of human happiness, which appears to be confirmed in subject responses to the threat of death from the air: see Moore, *Reflection on the Causes of Human Misery*.

5 See http://www.whittierdailynews.com/article/ZZ/20110220/NEWS/11 0229161.

6 See http://www.open.ac.uk/Arts/history-from-police-archives/RB1/Pt4/pt4Hurricane87.html.

7 http://www.nytimes.com/movie/review?res=9F01E3D8103CE63BBC40 52DFB467.

Chapter 7

1 'By close ups of the things around us, by focusing on hidden details of familiar objects, by exploring commonplace milieus under the ingenious guidance of the camera, the film, on the one hand, extends our comprehension of the necessities which rule our lives; on the other hand, it manages to assure us of an immense and unexpected field of action. ... With the close up, space expands, with slow motion, movement is extended. The enlargement of a snapshot does not simply render more precise what in any case was visible, though unclear: it reveals entirely new structural formations of the subject's impulses' (Benjamin 1973: 230). In the 1930s Benjamin was centrally concerned

with the parallel development of new technologies of killing and new technologies of both visual and auditory representation – radio, film, the gramophone and telephone – and the problematic moral issues that arose out of such a conjoining. This sensory mix has involved the simultaneous enhancement and restriction of the sensory experience of the world.

The transformation that technology had on the human sensorium and the attendant ethical implications of this was highlighted in the scepticism of the German philosopher Heidegger's understanding of sensory transformation embedded in media use. Heidegger pointed to the role of media technologies in abolishing, or creating cognitive confusion, in the experience of distance:

> The frantic abolition of all distances brings no nearness; for nearness does not consist in shortness of distance. What is least remote from us in point of distance, by virtue of its picture on film or its sound on the radio, can remain far from us. What is incalculably far from us in point of distance can be near to us. (Heidegger 1978)

Between Mumford and Turkle we have had a range of social theorists who have articulated the changing sensory landscape of the twentieth century, with Marshall McLuhan proclaiming in the 1960s that the world had become a 'global village', thereby replacing space, place and proximity, to Joshua Meyrowitz who claimed that

> Electronic media destroy the specialness of place and time. Television, radio, and telephone turn once private places into more public ones by making them more accessible to the outside world. ... Through such media, what is happening almost anywhere can be happening wherever we are. Yet when we are everywhere, we are also in no place in particular. (Meyrowitz 1987: 125)

In many ways these theorists were merely articulating the Heideggerian observation concerning technology.

2 Sounds imagined in the mind of readers exist with no vibrations. This is not the place to interrogate epistemologies of sound that are 'vibrational' but merely to point to the work of Grimshaw and Garner, who controversially assert that, 'all sound exists entirely in the mind and sound waves themselves are not sound. Within our definition, a sound wave can be a fundamental component of sound, but does not itself undergo transformation into sound. This does not mean that the cause of sound is entirely internal ... all perception is, in part determined by the external environment' (Grimshaw and Garner

2015: 115). The reader who imagines the seductive sound of Sirens and maybe their 'physical' appearance derives these 'imaginings' from a range of cultural messages and representations.

3 Benjamin's notion of an optical unconscious has become more literal in contemporary theorizing of the sensory nature of filmic engagement with the work of Marks (2002) and Elliott (2011) among others.

4 The case of Stormy Daniels arrested at the Sirens Gentleman's Club is discussed in chapter 11. See Daniels (2018).

5 The hi-fi soundscape is one in which 'discrete sounds can be heard clearly because of the low ambient noise level ... In the hi-fi soundscape, sounds overlap less frequently; there is perspective – foreground and background ... In a low-fi soundscape individual acoustic signals are obscured in an overdense population of sounds ... Perspective is lost ... there is no distance; only presence' (Schafer 1994: 43).

6 Archaeologists have associated the earliest human-headed bird creatures with the ancient Egyptian god Ba, who was also associated with death. There are also monuments from ancient Mesopotamia that depict birds with human heads that are associated with gods of the underworld, as in Egyptian myth. In these myths, people were brought to the underworld by birds/goddesses. In Greek culture itself the soul was sometimes thought to pass out of the mouth of the dying person in the form of a bird (see Havva and Bilson (2013)). The global exportation of the mermaid myth within popular culture is the subject of Hayward's 2018 book.

7 H. G. Wells's allusion to Herman Melville's novel *Moby Dick* is apparent here. A connection between Sirens and Melville's novel has also been made by Maurice Blanchot:

> Between Ahab and the whale there plays out a drama that could be called metaphysical in a vague sense of the word, the same struggle that is played out between the Sirens and Ulysses. Each of these pairs wants to be everything, wants to be the absolute world, which makes coexistence with the other absolute world impossible, and yet each one has no greater desire than this very coexistence, this encounter. To unite in the same space Ahab and the whale, the Sirens and Ulysses – that is the secret wish that makes Ulysses Homer, makes Ahab's Melville, and the world that results from this union the greatest, most terrible, and most beautiful of possible worlds, alas a book, nothing but a book. (Blanchot 2003: 5)

8 Typical of the Sirens as male sexual encounter in psychoanalysis is Golan's description, 'The myth of the sirens is a suitable metaphor

for the voice as *object a*. Their voices represent on the one hand pure desire, and on the other pure death. The Siren song binds its listeners in an obsessive way to the fascination of death. The jouissance derived from listening to its lethal jouissance' (Golan 2018: 97). While the identity of Homer's Sirens was ambiguous, although not so ambiguous for contemporary theorists to attribute their attraction to men, not as sound, but symbolically in terms of their genitalia. Of course, as Sirens migrated to the sea and gathered fishtails the male sexual imaginary would have to move to other parts of the Siren/woman's body. LaMay and Armstrong track these changes, which they argue are attributed to all female voices, not merely those of Sirens:

> Early modern theorists contrived that the female vocal chords, or uvula, were simply an oral variation of her vulva, another entrance point for the phallus. Her throat was likened to her uterus, and the clitoris was partner to the uvula on the grounds that both pieces of flesh controlled the heat of the "neck" to which they provided entry. When her uvula was undulating in the act of producing song she was considered especially 'hot', her mouth open in an explicit invitation for sex, and her uvula in a rapturous state of 'excessive jouissance'. (LaMay and Armstrong in Austern and Naroditskaya 2006: 318)

9 Meteorologists establishing America's first hurricane warning service after the tragedy at Galveston in 1900 and physicists tracking wind currents and air viscosity discovered what sailors already knew, that neither foghorns nor Joseph Henry's 'very large steam siren' nor eight huge megaphones, seventeen feet long with mouths seven feet wide, broadcasting the shrill of a steam whistle to all points of the compass could be affectively heard under foul conditions (Schwartz 2011: 509).

Chapter 8

1 Universalized sound can also be used for sinister purposes as in Jonestown in the 1970s, the site of the largest suicide in American history. Jones created a totalitarian sound world in the middle of the Guyanian jungle as Rebecca Layton, one of Jonestown's few survivors of the mass 1978 suicide, recounts, 'In Jonestown there was a speaker system and only Jim Jones spoke on it and it went 24 hours a day, and he would tape himself so – in the middle of the night – all through the night his voice was talking to you' (Layton 1988: 86).

Chapter 10

1 A seminal moment in the silencing of Sirens within popular culture arrives with the publication of Hans Christian Andersen's 'The Little Mermaid', written in 1836, itself a derivation of F. de la Motte Fouqué's *Undine*, published some twenty-five years earlier in 1811. Both stories are primarily concerned with the absence of a mermaid 'soul' and the mermaid's desire to attain one, as the path to everlasting life, though it is only available to a mermaid through the love of a man. The stories exist within a Christian ethos, especially Hans Christian Andersen's, and define mermaids/undines as 'other' but nevertheless redeemable if they succeed in obtaining a 'soul'. (This role is interestingly reversed in Oscar Wilde's short story 'The Fisherman and His Soul'.) These stories are of significance in terms of their gender stereotyping and their socializing role for young people of all sexes and as a cultural trace that is embodied in an array of Hollywood movies, including the Disney mermaid movies and the contemporary genre of Siren novels aimed at the same consumer market.

Chapter 12

1 Hillel Swartz concurs that the origin and audibility of sound at sea is fraught with difficulty: 'Meteorologists establishing America's first hurricane warning service after the tragedy at Galveston in 1900, and physicists tracking wind currents and air-viscosity discovered what sailors already knew, that neither foghorn nor Joseph Henry's "very large steam siren" nor eight huge megaphones, seventeen feet long with mouths seven feet wide, broadcasting the shrill of a steam whistle to all points of the compass could effectively be heard under foul conditions' (Schwartz 2011: 509).

2 This episode becomes a core element in Horkheimer's and Adorno's *Dialectic of Enlightenment*, of course, where they interpret the episode primarily in terms of class and culture whereby Odysseus represents the first bourgeois individual who experiences the sound of the Sirens as a form of sublimated desire – as art – while the poor rowers – the working class – are precluded from listening, but row on in silence – all body and muscle.

3 The *Oxford English Dictionary* – what else – defines 'Sirens' in multiple ways: 'Greek mythology. Any of several women or winged creatures, half woman half bird, whose singing was supposed to lure

unwary sailors to destruction on the rocks. Formerly also a mermaid. ... A woman who sings sweetly; a dangerously fascinating woman, a temptress; anything tempting or alluring' (*Shorter Oxford English Dictionary, Vol 2* 2007). Equally, LaMay and Armstrong claim that, 'whether or not she wants the label, women's singing in Western culture has been inextricably linked to her sexualized body, a body whose ambition is to seduce, and this relationship is what can denote her as siren' (LaMay and Armstrong in Austern and Naroditskaya 2006: 319).

4   Only on rare occasions have academics delved into the questionable assumptions surrounding the ambiguous gender messages sung out by Homer's Sirens, thus bringing the debate into the cultural climate of the twenty-first century. Of importance here is Judith Peraino's *Listening to the Sirens: Musical Technologies of Queer Identity from Homer to Hedweg* (2006).

5   H. G. Wells's novel *The Sea Lady* is one of the rare early novels that portray women as seeing and hearing a Siren. The story is set on the Folkstone coast and involves a family of the English upper-middle class holidaying on the coast. The story is striking in its habitual representation of a Victorian family together with their prejudices and sexual and social norms. The mermaid who appears off the Folkstone coast is observed in the first instance by the women in the family: 'and then they looked, and there, about thirty yards away was the Sea Lady's head, as if she were swimming back to land. ... The swimmer gave a queer sort of flop in the water, threw up her arm and vanished!' (Wells 1902 [2013]: vii). H. G. Wells's book appears as a template for the Siren movies of the 1940s. For example, in *Miranda* (1948) Glynis Johns plays a mermaid (Miranda) who pulls the hapless Paul Martin into the ocean off the Cornish coast while fishing. He awakes to find he is in Miranda's underwater cave. Miranda, a beautiful and playful young mermaid, entrances Martin, who agrees to take her back to land, specifically his London flat, where he arranges for Margaret Rutherford, who plays an eccentric nurse, to look after her. The film is a series of enticements as Miranda flirts with and entices the three main male characters in the film. Miranda hides her tail with clothes, maintaining the front as a young invalid just as in Wells's novel.

6   It was Apollonius of Rhodes writing some 300 years after Homer who described the Sirens as 'half-birds – half women' in *Jason and the Golden Fleece*, creatures of the sky rather than the sea (Appollonius of Rhodes 1993: 119). While the story itself is said to pre-date Homer, visual data depicting Sirens as 'half-bird, half woman' are dated during the time of *Jason and the Golden Fleece* rather than the *Odyssey*. The wonderful example of a Siren vase held in the British Museum in

London is dated at 480 BCE, for example, some 300 years after the writing of the *Odyssey*.

7 The following critique of the Li Galli experiments should not be read as a critique of media archaeology itself. Indeed, the present work might be construed as a form of media archaeology, but allied more to the earlier work of the Frankfurt School in the form of the *Dialectic of Enlightenment* coupled with a sympathetic, yet differing, take on Ernst Bloch's notion of cultural and historical traces (Bloch (2006) and Horkheimer and Adorno (1972 [2007]). There is much excellent work undertaken theoretically and empirically from a media archaeology perspective, not least from the pen of Wolfgang Ernst (2014), Till (2014) and others.

8 Kittler frequently referred to the music of Pink Floyd in his writing, more often than not *The Piper at the Gates of Dawn*. See Winthrop-Young (2006).

9 Sisyphus, the Greek God condemned to push his rock up a mountain only to watch it fall down again. On watching the rock return to whence it came, Albert Camus surmised that in that moment, Sisyphus is resigned to his fate – and must assume that he is happy (Camus 2018).

BIBLIOGRAPHY

1992 BBC Wartime Broadcasting Service Script. Never Aired. news.bbc.co.uk/1/shared/bsp/hi/pdfs/03_10_08nuclearattack.pdf

Adorno, T. (May–June 1980) 'Bloch's "Traces": The Philosophy of Kitsch'. *New Left Review*, vol. 1, no. 121, pp. 1–9.

Adorno, T. (2005a) *Catchwords and Interventions*. New York: Columbia University Press.

Adorno, T. (2005b) *Minima Moralia. Reflections on Damaged Life*. London: Verso.

Altman, R. (1980) 'Moving Lips: Cinema as Ventriloquism'. *Yale French Studies*, no. 60, pp. 67–79.

Appolinius of Rhodes. (1993) *Jason and the Golden Fleece* (Trans. Richard Hunter) Oxford: Oxford University Press.

Aragon, L. (1999) *Paris Peasant*. London: Exact Change, Reprint Editions.

Aratani, L. (22 February 2019). *Guardian*. Accessed 13 June. https://www.theguardian.com/us-news/2019/feb/22/new-york-sirens-noise-police-fire-ambulance.

Auerbach, N. (1982) *Woman and the Demon: The Life of a Victorian Myth*. Cambridge: Harvard University Press.

Austern, L. and Inna Naroditskaya. (2006) *Music of the Sirens*. Bloomington: Indiana University Press.

Barrington Moore, Jr. (1922) *Reflection on the Causes of Human Misery*. London: Allen Lane.

Benjamin, W. (1973) *Illuminations*. London: Penguin Books.

Birdsall, C. (2012) *Nazi Soundscapes: Sound, Technology and Urban Space in Germany, 1933–1945*. Amsterdam: Amsterdam University Press.

Blanchot, M. (2003) *Encountering the Imaginary in The Book to Come*. Stanford: Stanford University Press.

Bloch, E. (1986) *The Principle of Hope*. Cambridge: Blackwell Press.

Bloch, E. (2006) *Traces*. Stanford: Stanford University Press.

Boa, E. (1 January 2004) 'Revoicing Silenced Sirens: A Changing Motif in the Works by Franz Kafka, Frank Wedekind and Barbara Kohler'. *German Life and Letters*, vol. 57, pp. 1–26.

Borbach, C. (2016) 'Siren Songs and Echo's Response: Towards a Media Theory of the Voice in the Light of Speech Synthesis'. On_Culture: The Open Journal for the Study of Culture, vol. 2. http://geb.uni-giessen.de/geb/volltexte/2016/12354/.
Bradford, E. (2004) *Ulysses Found*. Stroud: Sutton Publishing.
Bull, M. (2000) *Sounding Out the City: Personal Stereos and the Management of Everyday Life*. London: Berg.
Bull, M. (2007) *Sound Moves: iPod Culture and Urban Experience*. London: Routledge.
Bull, M. (2018) *The Routledge Companion to Sound Studies*. London: Routledge.
Camus, A. (2018) *The Myth of Sisyphus*. Stroud: Dutton/Signet. Originally published in French 1942.
Canetti, E. (2012) *Kafka's Other Trial*. London: Penguin Press.
Cass, K. (2016) *The Siren*. London: Harper Collins.
Cavarero, A. (2005) *For More Than One Voice: Towards a Philosophy of Vocal Expression*. Stanford: Stanford University Press.
Clement, C. *Opera and the Undoing of Women*. London: Virago Press.
Cohen, B. (1995) *The Distaff Side: Representing the Female in Homers Odyssey*. Oxford: Oxford University Press.
Cohen, L. (2016) 'You Want It Darker', Columbia Records 2016.
Comay, R. (2000) 'Adorno's Siren Song'. *New German Critique*, no. 81, pp. 21–48.
Corbin, A. (1998) *Village Bells: Sounds and Meaning in the Nineteenth-Century French Countryside*. New York: Columbia University Press.
Daniels, S. (2018) *Full Disclosure*. London: Macmillan.
Davis, T. (2007) *Stages of Emergency: Cold War Nuclear Civil Defense*. Durham: Duke University Press.
Daughtry, J. (2015) *Listening to War: Sound, Music, Trauma, and Survival in Wartime Iraq*. Oxford: Oxford University Press.
Davis, T. (2007) *Stages of Emergency: Cold War Nuclear Civil Defence*. Durham: Duke University Press
Dijkstra, B. (1986) *Idols of Perversity: Fantasies of Feminine Evil in Fin-De-Siecle Culture*. Oxford: Oxford University Press.
Dolar, M. (2006) *A Voice and Nothing More*. Cambridge: MIT.
Douglas, N. (2010) *Siren Land: A Celebration of Life in Southern Italy*. London: Tauris Parke.
Drake, D. (2015) *Paris at War 1939–1944*. Cambridge: Harvard University Press.
Duford, R. (Fall 2017) 'Daughters of the Enlightenment: Reconstructing Adorno on Gender and Feminist Praxis'. *Hypatia*, vol. 32, no. 4, pp. 784–800.
Elliott, P. (2011) *Hitchcock and the Cinema of Sensations: Embodied Film Theory and Cinematic Reception*. London: I. B. Tauris.

Epstein, J. (2014) *Sublime Noise: Musical Culture and the Modernist Writer*. Baltimore: Johns Hopkins University Press.

Ernst, W. (2014a) 'Towards a Media-Archaeology of Sirenic Articulations: Listening with Media Archaeological Ears'. *The Nordic Journal of Aesthetics*, no. 48, pp. 7–17.

Ernst, W. (2014b) 'Tracing Tempor(e)alities in the Age of Media Mobility'. *Media Theory*, vol. 2, no. 1, pp. 1–31.

Evangelista, M. and Henry Shue (eds) (2014) *The American Way of Bombing: Changing Ethical and Legal Norms, from Flying Fortresses to Drones*. Ithaca: Cornell University Press.

Euchner, M. (Spring 2012) 'The Ring's, Rhinemaidens: Singing Seductresses or Women of Wisdom?' *The Musical Times*, vol. 153, no. 1918, pp. 37–51.

Feulner, N. and Nadia Durrani. (2008) *In Search of the Zeppelin War: The Archeology of the First Blitz*. Chalford Stroud: Tempus Publishing.

Fleeger, J. (2014) *Mismatched Women: The Siren's Song through the Machine*. Oxford: Oxford University Press.

Fouqué, F. D. M. (1930) *Undine*. New York: Limited Editions Club.

Friedrich, J. (2006) *The Fire: The Bombing of Germany 1940–1945*. New York: Columbia University Press.

Frommolt, K. and M. Carle. (2014) 'The Song of the Sirens'. *The Nordic Journal of Aesthetics*, no. 48, pp. 18–33.

Gellen, K. (2019) *Kafka and Noise: The Discovery of Cinematic Sound in Literary Modernism*. Evanston: University of Illinois Press.

Golan, R. (2018) *Loving Psychoanalysis: Looking at Culture with Freud and Lacan*. London: Routledge.

Gibson, E. (2005) *The Original Million Dollar Mermaid: The Annette Kellerman Story*. London: Allen Unwin.

Gilbert, S. (2005) *Music in the Holocaust: Confronting Life in the Nazi Ghettos and Camps*. Oxford: Clarendon press.

Gorbea, G. (2015) Alert Fatigue Mexico city Residents Bombarded with Earhtquake Warings. https:// www.vice.com/en-us/article/9kjkvy/alert-fatique-mexic-city-residents-bombarded-with-earthquake-warnin.

Goux, J. J. (1990) *Symbolic Economies: After Marx and Freud*. Ithaca: Cornell University Press.

Grayzel, S. (2012) *At Home and Under Fire: Air Raids and Culture in Britain from the Great War to the Blitz*. Cambridge: Cambridge University Press.

Grimshaw, M. and Tom Garner (2015) *Sonic Virtuality: Sound as Emergent Perception*. Oxford: Oxford University Press.

Guehenno, J. (2014) *Diary of the Dark Years, 1940–1944*. Oxford: Oxford University Press.

Heidegger, M. (1978) *Basic Writings*. London: Routledge.

Havva, K. and O. Bilsen. (2013) Sirens as Soul Bearers on Lycian Grave Reliefs in the Classical Period'. *Cedrus*, vol. 1, pp. 89–105.

Hayward, P. (ed.). (2018) *Scaled for Success: The Internationalisation of the Mermaid*. London: John Libbey Publishing.
Hennessy, P. (2011) *The Secret State. Preparing for the Worst, 1945–2010*. London: Penguin Books.
Hersey, J. (2001) *Hiroshima*. London: Penguin Books.
Hewitt, A (Spring–Summer 1992) 'A Feminine Dialectic of Enlightenment? Horkheimer and Adorno Revisited'. *New German Critique*, no. 56, pp. 143–70.
Hod, I. (7 December 2014) *Israeli App Red Alert Saves lives -But It Just Might Drive You Nuts in Daily Beast*. https://www.thedailybeast.com/the-israeli-app-red-alert-saves-livesbut-it-just-might-drive-you-nuts.
Homer. (2017) *Odyssey* (trans Wilson). London: W. W. Norton and Co.
Horkheimer, M. and T. Adorno (2007) *Dialectic of Enlightenment*. Palo Alto: Stanford University Press.
Horstvedt, B. (October 2007). Review of Bloch, Ernst, *Traces*. H-German, H-Net Reviews. http://www.h-net.org/reviews/showrev.php?id=13778.
Horkheimer, M. and Theodor Adorno (1972) *Dialectic of Enlightenment*. London: Allen Lane.
Huscher, P. (1995). Chicago Symphony Orchestra Programme Notes. https://cso.org/uploadedFiles/1_Tickets_and_Events/Program_Notes/ProgramNotes_Varese_Ionisation.pdf.
Kafka, F. (2005) *The Complete Short Stories*. London: Vintage Books.
Kahles, W. (1976) 'Strabo and Homer: The Homeric Citations in the Geography of Strabo'. Paper 1596. http://ecommons.luc.edu/luc_diss/1596.
Kahn, D. (2001) *Noise, Water, Meat: A History of Sound in the Arts*. Cambridge: MIT Press.
Kane, B. (2014) *Sound Unseen: Acousmatic Sound in Theory and Practice*. Oxford: Oxford University Press.
Kaplan, D. (2009) 'The Song of the Siren: Engineering National Time on Israeli Radio'. *Cultural Anthropology*, vol. 24, no. 2, pp. 313–45.
Keskinen, M. (2008). *Audio Book: Essays on Sound Technologies in Narrative Fiction*, Lanham, MD: Lexington Books.
Knell, H. (2003) *To Destroy a City: Strategic Bombing and Its Human Consequences in World War Two*. Boston: De Capo Press.
Kracauer, S. (1995) *The Mass Ornament: Weimar Essays*. Cambridge: Harvard University Press.
Lagouranis, T. (2007) *Fear Up Harsh: An Army interrogator's Dark Journey Through Iraq*. London: Penguin Books.
Lamb, C. (1808) *The Adventures of Ulysses*. London: Edward Moxon.
Langer, D. (2017) *Siren Sisters*. New York: Aladdin.
Leach, E. (May 2006) 'The Little Pipe Sings Sweetly While the Fowler Deceives the Bird': Sirens in the Later Middle Ages'. *Music and Letters*, vol. 87, no. 2, pp. 187–211.

Le Breton, D. (2017) *Sensing the World: An Anthropology of the Senses*. London: Bloomsbury.
La May, T. and R. Armstrong (2006) 'The Navel, the Corporate, the Contradictory: Pop Sirens at the Twenty-first Century'. In *Music of the Sirens*, ed. L. Austern and Inna Naroditskaya. Bloomington: Indiana University Press.
Layton, D. (1988) *Seductive Poison: A Jonestown Survivor's Story of Life and Death in the Peoples Temple*. New York: Random Press.
Levi, P. (1991) *If This in a Man/The Truce*. London: Abacus.
Levy, I. (2006) *Sirens on the Western Shore: The Western Femme Fatale, Translation, and Vernacular Style in Modern Japanese Literature*. New York: Columbia University Press.
Liska, V. (2004) 'Two Sirens Singing: Literature as Contestation in Maurice Blanchot and Theodor W. Adorno'. *The Power of Contestation: Perspectives on Maurice Blanchot*. Baltimore: Johns Hopkins University Press.
Marben, R. (1931) *Zeppelin Adventures*. London: John Hamilton.
Marcuse, H. (2002) *One Dimensional Man*. London: Routledge.
Marks, L. (2002) *Touch: Sensuous Theory and Multisensory Media*. Minnesota: University of Minnesota Press.
Mathes, C. (2015) *Imagine the Sound: Experimental African American Literature after Civil Rights*. Minneapolis: University of Minnesota Press.
McCarthy, T. (2011) *Kittler and the Sirens*. London Review of Books blog, https://www.lrb.co.uk/blog/2011/november/kittler-and-the-sirens accessed September 16th 2017.
Meyrowitz, J. (1987) *No Sense of Place: The Impact of the Electronic Media on Social Behaviour*. Oxford: Oxford University Press.
Miklitsch, R. (2011) *Siren City: Sound and Source Music in Classic American Noir*. New Brunswick: Rutgers University Press.
Neuhaus, M. (rev. 1993) 'Sirens', accessed 14 February 2016, http://www.max-neuhaus.info/soundworks/vectors/invention/sirens/Sirens.pdf.
Neuhaus, M. (2003) 'Sirens'. Republished on http://www.max-neuhaus.info/bibliography.
Noesner, G. (2010) *Stalling for Time, My Life as an FBI Hostage Negotiator*. New York: Random House.
Nussbaum, M. (2001) *The Fragility of Goodness: Luck, Ethics in Greek Tragedy and Philosophy*. Cambridge: Cambridge University Press.
Osborne, R. *The London Consortium Static*. Issue 6 – Alarm, Alarms on Record.
Ovid. (2001) *The Metamorphoses of Ovid*. Boston: University of Massachusetts Press.
Peraino, J. (2006) *Listening to the Sirens: Musical Technologies of Queer Identity from Homer to Hedwig*. Berkeley: University of California Press.

Pieslack, J. (2009) *Sound Targets: American Soldiers and Music in the Iraq War*. Bloomington: Indiana University Press.

Plato. (1944) *The Republic*. New York: Limited Editions Club.

Pucci, P. (1998) *The Song of the Sirens, Essays on Homer*. Lanham: Rowman and Littlefield Publisher.

Quignard, P. (2016) *The Hatred of Music*. New Haven: Yale University Press.

Rath, R. C. (2003) *How Early America Sounded*. Ithaca: Cornell University Press.

Reavis, D. (1995) *The Ashes of Waco: An Investigation*. New York: Simon and Shuster.

Reniere, F. ///Users/fafd1/Desktop/Sirens/Young/Boyandthe"Good"War WWIINetherlandsEscapeLines.webarchive. Accessed 16 June 2016.

Richards, F. M. (2016) *'Dangerous Creatures': Selected Children's Versions of Homer's Odyssey in English 1699–2014*. Durham theses, Durham University. Available at Durham E-Theses. Online: http//etheses.dur.ac.uk/11522/.

Rosbottom, R. (2015) *When Paris Went Dark: The City of Light under German Occupation, 1940–44*. London: John Murray.

Ross, A. (27 July 2016). 'When Music Is Violence'. *New Yorker*. https://www.newyorker.com/magazine/2016/07/04/when-music-is-violence.

Ross, J. (9 April 2015). Wisconsin village votes to keep daily sirens in Star Tribune. www.startribune.com/wisconsin-village-votes-to-keep-daily-sirens/299069721/.

Schafer, M. (1994) The *Soundscape: Our Sonic Environment and the Tuning of the World*. Rochester: Destiny.

Schmidt, L. (2000) *Hearing Things: Religion, Illusion and the American Enlightenment*. Cambridge, MA: Harvard University Press.

Schofield, J. (2014) 'The Archaeology of Sound and Music'. *World Archaeology*, vol. 46, no. 3, pp. 289–91.

Schwartz, H. (2011) *Making Noise: From Babel to the Big Bang & Beyond*. New York: Zone Books.

Schweighauser, P. (2006) *The Noises of American Literature, 1890–1985: Toward a History of Literary Acoustics*. Gainesville: The University Press of Florida.

Sconce, J. (2000) *Haunted Media: Electronic Presence from Telegraphy to Television*. Durham: Duke University Press.

Segal, C. (1994) *Singer, Heroes, and Gods in the Odyssey*. Ithaca: Cornell University Press.

Shattuck, R. (1996) *Forbidden Knowledge: From Prometheus to Pornography*. New York: St Martin's Press.

Sloterdijk, P. (2011) *Spheres Volume1: Bubbles, Microspherology*. Cambridge: MIT Press.

Smart, M. A. (2000) *Siren Songs: Representation of Gender and Sexuality in Opera*. Princeton: Princeton University Press.

Smirnov, A. (2013) *Sound in Z: Experiments in Sound and Electronic Music in Early 20th Century Russia*. Berlin: Buchhandling Walther Konis GmbH and Co.

Smith, B. (1999) *The Acoustic World of Early Modern England: Attending to the O-Factor*. Chicago: The University of Chicago Press.

Stach, R. (2016) *Is That Kafka? 99 Finds*. New York: New Directions Books.

Strabo. (2014) *The Geography of Strabo* (Trans Roller). Cambridge: Cambridge University Press.

St. Clair, J. (2013) *Sound and Aural Media in Postmodern Literature: Novel Listening*. New York: Routledge.

St. Clair, J. (2018) 'Literature and Sound'. In *The Routledge Companion to Sound Studies*, ed. M. Bull. London: Routledge.

Stoever, J. (2016) *The Sonic Color Line: Race and the Politics of Listening*. New York: New York University Press.

Taylor, F. (2004) *Dresden: Tuesday 13 February 1945*. London: Bloomsbury Press.

Taylor, F. (2015) *Coventry, Thursday, 14 November 1940*. London: Bloomsbury Press.

Teodorski, M. (2016) *Through the Siren's Looking Glass: Victorian Monstrosity of the Male Desiring Subject*, Unpublished Doctorate, University of Tubingen.

Till, R. (2014) 'Sound Archaeology: Terminology, Palaeolithic Cave Art and Soundscape'. *World Archaeology*, vol. 46, no. 3, pp. 292–304.

Van Lengen (2016) *Why Are There 'So Many Sirens' in D.C.?* Accessed at https://wamu.org/story/16/01/28/why_are_there_so_many_sirens_in_dc/.

Van Liefferinge, C. (2012) 'Sirens: From the Deadly Song to the Music of the Spheres. Homeric Readings and Platonic interpretations'. *Revue De L'Histoire Des Religions*, vol. 229, no. 4pp. 128ff.

Vonnegut, K. (1999) *The Sirens of Titan*. London: Orion Books.

Vonnegut, K. (2006) *A Man Without a Country*. London: Bloomsbury Press.

Vonnegut, K. (2019) *Slaughterhouse Five or The Children's Crusade*. London: Vintage Classics. Fatal Force. https://washingtonpost.com/graphics/2019/national/police-shootings -2019/.

Weiss, H. (2014) *Helga's Diary: A Young Girl's Account of Life in a Concentration Camp*. London: Penguin Books.

Wellmer, A. (2000) 'The Death of the Sirens and the Origin of the Work of Art'. *New German Critique*, no. 81, pp. 5–19.

Wells, H. G. (2013) *The Sea Lady*. London: Hardpress Publishing.

Wilson, M. (29 July 2004) '80 Sirens Wailing, But Do Not Panic: This Is Only a Drill'. *New York Times*.

White, J. (2014) *Zeppelin Nights: London in the First World War*. London: Bodley Head Press.

Winthrop-Young, G. (2006) 'Implosion and Intoxication. Kittler, A German Classic, and Pink Floyd'. *Theory, Culture and Society*, vol. 23, nos 7–8, pp. 75–91.

Winthrop-Young, G. *Kittler's Siren Recursions*. Accessed 7 September 2017, https://monoskop.org/images/4/42/WinthropYoung_Geoffrey_Kittlers_Siren_Recursions.pdf.

Zachary, M. (2011) *The Lost Books of the Odyssey*. London: Vintage Press.

Zayaruznaya, A. (2018) *The Monstrous New Art: Divided Forms in the Late Medieval Motet*. Cambridge: Cambridge University Press.

INDEX

acousmatic 12, 18–24, 68, 87–9, 98
Adorno, Theodor 4, 10, 26, 36, 47–8, 61, 71, 75, 97, 109–10, 114
Alice, Wolf 6, 114
Altman, Rick 18
Andersen, Hans Christian 8, 29, 81–3, 85, 87, 90–1, 111, 121
Antheil, George 19
Apollonius of Rhodes 28, 68–9
Aristotle 30
auditory imagination 16, 22
Austern, Linda 12, 24, 29, 109
Avraamov, Arseny 59–60

Bach, J. S. 25–6
Bauer, Felice 90–1
Beckett, Samuel 7
bells 10, 58–9, 76–7
Benjamin, Walter 119–18
Birdsall, Carolyn 44
Black Lives Matter 57
Blanchot, Maurice 15, 87, 119
Bloch, Ernst 9–11, 33, 114, 123
Borges, Jorge Luis 15
Branch Davidians 34–5
Branford, Ernie 103–5
Buckley, Tim 113

Camus, Albert 123
Canetti, Elias 90–1

Cass, Kiera 82–3
Caveraro, Adriana 8
Chion, Michel 19
Clanvowe, John 105
Clement, Catherine 25–6, 33
Cohen, Leonard 86, 108
Cohen, Beth 4
Comay, Rebecca 71
Corbin, Alain 58, 77

Daniels, Stormy 10, 94–6
Dante, Aligieri 28
Daughtry, Martin 39
Debussy, Claude 6
Dijkstra, Bram 11, 23, 33, 90, 109
Disney, Walt 10, 81–2, 87, 111
Dohert, Lillian 110
Dolar, Mladen 8
Douglas, Norman 103
Dresden 15–16, 35, 42, 62–3, 114–15
Duford, Rochelle 110

Ellman, Paul 56–7
Enlightenment
  Adorno, Theodor and Max Horkheimer 9, 17, 28
  dialectics 6, 10, 17
  ideology 26
  instrumental rationality 17, 26
  masculinity 9
Epstein, Josh 19

INDEX

Ernst, Wolfgang 98–9, 102
Euchner, Marie 34–5, 115

Fénelon 83–4
Fouqué, De La Motte 82

Gellen, Kata 86–9
Goethe, Johann Wolfgang von 27
Guehenno, Jean 40

Hayward, Philip 119
Heraclitus 23
Hersey, John 74–5
Hewitt, Andrew 110
Hiroshima 44, 68, 74
Homer 4, 10, 28, 61, 71, 82, 94, 113
   Circe 20–1
   Odyssey 5, 8, 11, 15, 20–2
   Scylla 22
honey
   Greek thought 21–3
   Homer 21–2
Horkheimer, Max 4

Ihde, Don 16

Jonestown 120
Joyce, James 6, 114

Kafka, Franz 6, 10, 87–93, 98, 106, 111
Kane, Brian 19–20
Kaplan, Danny 79
Kellermann, Annette 67, 108, 111–12
Keppler, Johannes 31
Kittler, Frederik 10, 97–107
Knell, Herman 44, 47

Lamb, Charles 84–5
Lang, Fritz 8

Langer, Dana 81–2
Leach, Elizabeth Eva 29, 31
Le Breton, David 18
Liefferinge, Catherine 22, 72
listening 5, 9, 16, 20, 36, 45, 56, 67
   racialization of 57–8, 86

McLuhan, Marshall 7, 118
Marcuse, Herbert 110
masculinity 10
Mellors, Wilfred 25, 27
Metallica 115
Monroe, Marilyn 30
music
   for the dead 31
   hip-hop 38
   as jamming technology 28
   musicology 4
   muzac 37
   sexual violence 27–8, 32–3
   spheres 31
   utopian 26
musical instruments
   lyre 28, 69

Neuhaus, Max 116
noise 19
Noise abatement societies 5, 7

opera 23
   gender and violence 23
Ovid 23, 28, 32–4, 98

Peraino, Judith 4, 7, 122
phenomenology 19, 57
Pieslak, Jonathan 115
Pink, Floyd 106–7, 123
Plato 30, 98
   myth of Er 23, 31, 64, 72
   Neoplatonism 31
   Republic 23, 30, 72–3

Quignard, Pascal 8

Rascal, Dizzee 6, 57, 60
Rath, Richard 9

Sartre, Jean-Paul 29
Schaeffer Pierre 19
Schafer, Murray 76–7
Schoenberg, Arnold 59
Schwartz, Hillel 5–6, 121
senses 19
   multi-sensory 18
   overload 46
   training 44–7
sight 16
silence 40, 86
   and destruction 43
   women 26
Sinatra, Nancy 35
sirens
   air-raid 4, 6, 36–52, 73
   birds 8
   body 8, 12, 18, 30
   cyborg 8
   definitions 6–8
   enlightenment 6
   factory 58–9
   funeral rites 31
   gender 4, 6, 23, 70
   hearing 16
   Hollywood 8, 11, 16, 74, 98, 109, 111
   ideology 16, 47–52
   industrialization 5, 76–80
   knowledge 10
   mermaids 6, 70, 81, 105
   myth 6, 8, 15–16, 23, 27
   nature 17
   nymphs 32, 84–5, 89
   police 39, 41
   popular culture 4
   Rhinemaidens 27, 33–4, 115
   sexuality 7, 27, 29–30

silencing 9, 11, 67, 82, 87–93, 94–6, 110
smart 4
song 8
urban 53–60
Victorian culture 6, 23, 30, 90–1
visualizing 16, 24, 30
voice 5, 8, 9, 84, 87, 92–3
war 11, 14–16
Sloterdijk, Peter 9–10, 26–7, 31, 72, 98, 105
Smith, Mark 57
sonic archaeology 98, 106
sound
   acousmatic 18–24
   aesthetics 59–60
   engineer 20
   engulfing 55
   imaginary 18
   indeterminacy 42
   industrial 5, 8–9
   mechanical 7
   nostalgia 7
   phenomenology of 19
   siren 10
   space 38–40, 53, 70
   vibration 67, 75
   walks 19
soundscapes 4, 40, 68, 76–80, 98
sound waves 9
Stach, Reiner 91
Sterne, Jonathan 24
Strabon 10, 100

technologies
   destructiveness 36–52
   radar 41
   radio 47, 98
   smartphones 37, 39, 52, 67 80
   telephone 41, 98

trains 78–9
Walkman 106–7
Teodorski, Marco 30
time 61–6
   knowledge 10, 12
Twin Towers 53–4

Varese, Edgard 38, 59–60
vibrations 11
Virgil 23
Vonnegut, Kurt 10, 15–17, 61–6, 78, 114

Wagner, Richard 27, 33–4, 89, 115
weapons
   intercontinental ballistic missile 20
Wellmer, Albrecht 27, 71
Wells, H. G. 70–1, 98, 119
World War I 6, 20, 39, 45, 46
World War II 4, 37, 39, 41, 42, 45–8, 78, 79, 103, 104

Zayaruznaya, Anna 4